A COLONIAL SOUTHERN BOOKSHELF

A COLONIAL
SOUTHERN
BOOKSHELF

*Reading in the
Eighteenth Century*

RICHARD BEALE DAVIS

*MERCER UNIVERSITY
LAMAR MEMORIAL LECTURES
No. 21*

THE UNIVERSITY OF GEORGIA PRESS

ATHENS

Copyright © 1979 by the University of Georgia Press
Athens, Georgia 30602

Set in 10 on 13 point VariTyper Baskerville
Printed in the United States of America

Library of Congress Cataloging in Publication Data

Davis, Richard Beale.
   A colonial Southern bookshelf.
   (Mercer University Lamar memorial lectures; no. 21)
   Includes index.
   1. Books and reading—Southern States—History—18th
century.   2. Southern States—Intellectual life—Colonial
period, ca. 1600–1775.   I. Title.   II. Series: Mercer University, Macon, Ga. Lamar memorial lectures; no. 21.

Z1003.3.S85D38   028′.9   78–3832

ISBN 0-8203-0450-6

FOR
V.D.B. AND E.D.W.

Contents

Foreword

RICHARD BEALE DAVIS, THE PREEMINENT SCHOLAR OF EARLY
southern literature, has provided a fitting conclusion to the
"series within the series" with which the Lamar Lectures at
Mercer University have marked the nation's bicentennial. Em-
ploying the results of his vast research and the research of
others, and his wonderfully wide and deep familiarity with
eighteenth-century ideas, Professor Davis has given us a description of the books southerners read in the period leading
up to and including the Revolution; he also makes several
suggestions as to how these books help us to understand the
early southern mind. To have heard these lectures, as we at
Mercer have, or to read this book, is to explore an interesting
and relatively neglected part of the history of ideas in the
South.

Landon Carter, inscribing a book of Virginia laws he was
presenting to his son in 1769, wrote, "This volume contains
the Laws of your Country, and . . . no Gentleman should be
ignorant of them." This was a characteristic attitude in the
southern colonies, as Professor Davis demonstrates, and he
goes on to suggest how southern reading in law and government shaped and reflected the minds of the many southerners
who created this nation.

Examining religious books common to southern colonial
bookshelves, Professor Davis provides support for recent con-
tentions that the southern colonists were not as indifferent to
religion as previous scholars have claimed. An admirable

range of doctrines was studied by eighteenth-century southerners, and their tolerance seems more the product of balance than
of apathy.

In their reading of belles lettres the southerners seem different from other colonial Americans in their greater preference
for humor and for dramatic literature, whether performed on
the stage or read by the family at fireside. Professor Davis
perceives that these preferences may well foreshadow the nature of that robust literature that was to spring forth in the
southern renascence of the twentieth century.

Richard Beale Davis's meticulous scholarship has demonstrated here, as in his other works, the liveliness and compre-
hensiveness of the early southern mind. In accomplishing this
he has ably fulfilled the intentions of Mrs. Eugenia Dorothy
Blount Lamar, whose bequest established and maintains this
lecture series as a medium for the study of southern culture.
The Lamar Memorial Lectures Committee is grateful to Professor Davis for his fine contribution.

Michael Cass
for the Lamar Memorial Lectures Committee

A COLONIAL SOUTHERN BOOKSHELF

Introduction

THE ESTABLISHMENT OF THE LAMAR LECTURES IN ITSELF SEEMS to imply qualities shared in common throughout the southern region and continuity in its culture. Many previous writer-contributors have rightly considered aspects of the area's most intellectually distinguished period, the twentieth century. Others have traced modes or aspects of its literary and political and social heritage back from our age to 1800. Quite recently at least two of my distinguished predecessors in this series, inspired in part by our national bicentennial, have been concerned with the Colonial and Revolutionary aspects of the southern mind, facets of a culture interesting enough in themselves but more significant as the first examples of a continuing and surviving intellectual character. Professors Peterson and Greene have noted, for example, the pervasiveness of historical consciousness in the political and economic thinking of the eighteenth-century South, a consciousness that most of us know survives in themes and attitudes in the novels, poems, and plays composed in the region even in the last two generations.

The present lectures proceed from this assumption of a degree of southern intellectual continuity and a degree of southern unity in the diversity of its mind, assumptions frequently only implicit in these discussions. They endeavor to indicate the nature or character of early southern thinking through a look at some of the things read in the coastal area from Maryland through Georgia in the eighteenth century. The titles and content of this printed material, its popularity or frequency of use, and its accessibility suggest a number of things about those who read it and what they did.

Suggest is almost all that this brief examination of colonial southern libraries can do. It can offer no final answers about general literacy and literary taste, about general familiarity with written English and provincial law, or about the relative liberalism or conservatism, theologically or politically or socially, of even the owners or borrowers of books. For one thing, all of the existing evidence has not even been made available, much less examined. Older states, as generally historically conscious as Maryland and South Carolina, and to some extent Virginia and North Carolina and Georgia, admit that hundreds of inventory booklists are still buried in their official manuscript records. State- or privately sponsored historical societies acknowledge that, perhaps, for every published booklist from their archives there is another in manuscript, relatively or wholly unknown even to intellectual historians. Only now is a scholar gathering printed sales catalogues of eighteenth-century books held by commercial vendors or the administrators of private estates. Many of them are southern, and almost all were unknown two decades ago. Yet to be discovered is a copy of the contemporary, known-to-have-been-printed catalogue of the greatest colonial southern library, that of the three William Byrds—and the one printing within the last century from an eighteenth-century manuscript inadvertently omits a considerable number of titles. All of these lists, preferably with their (usually) short titles expanded, must be printed or reprinted before even qualified conclusions may be drawn.

Any conclusions from all this material would still be qualified or limited for there are abundant clues—but no more—to the onetime existence of many other libraries, large and small and very small, among southern colonial men and women. For example, not a single title is now known, except by inference from his writings, of the large book collection of South Carolina Chief Justice Nicholas Trott, one of the genuinely learned men of eighteenth-century America. An inventory of the possessions of an erudite planter-lawyer which notes simply "a study of books," or another of a William and Mary professor of "a study full of books," is exasperating and tantalizing. Perhaps more significant as suggestions of various stages of literacy are the entries, usually but not always in the inventories of the southern middle class (small merchants and planters and skilled artisans and "inferior clergy"), of "a parcel of books," "a parcel of old books," "sixty old French and Latin books," or "six religious books."

That many apprentices and indentured servants and, at intervals and at various places, blacks, slave and free, were taught to read and write suggests greater literacy among the lower classes than is generally known or admitted, and it also suggests that these people might have owned a few books. The records of the Society for the Propagation of the Gospel in Foreign Parts, of the Society for the Propagation of Christian Knowledge, and of Dr. Bray's Associates contain lists of Bibles and prayer books and Testaments and devotional manuals which were distributed in large numbers—and, one may be fairly sure, not usually presented gratis to the upper classes. And manuals for house builders, shipwrights, and carpenters seem to have been intended for artisans and their apprentices as well as for supervisors, plantation owners or city merchants. Perhaps fairly accurate figures as to the proportion of book owners and readers among the various social classes can hardly be arrived at, but recent studies of colonial literacy, already or soon to be in print, suggest that many people had at least a few books, people including the Scotch-Irish piedmont and mountain frontiersmen and the Indian traders who spent most of their lives in the southern Appalachians. To see the traders as literate or learned, one should read such books as the great history of the red man by James Adair or the recently published records of Indian affairs in the colony of South Carolina.

That some suggestions can be made of the character of the eighteenth-century southern mind is evident from the scores of booklists already available in print or easily accessible manuscript and from the literary allusions and obviously borrowed ideas in the substantial body of printed writing by southerners of the century. In state historical journals, perhaps most frequently in Virginia, dozens or perhaps scores of library inventories have already been published—large, medium, and small. The published catalogues of the Charleston Library Society of 1750 and 1770 and the Library Company of Baltimore of 1798 are extensive and enlightening. The 1798 Maryland catalogue contains not only 62 pages of book titles but an interesting list of members and the constitution and general statement of aims of this private circulating library. Then there are the recently unearthed sales catalogues, such as that for 1796(?) issued by Bailey and Waller of Charleston with 33 pages of book titles. Easily accessible in the Virginia State Library is a 1797 manuscript inventory of books for sale in a country store in entirely rural Lunenburg County; it is a surprisingly sophisticated list. Perhaps above all is the five-volume annotated *Catalogue of the Library of Thomas Jefferson,* printed in the 1950s, a catalogue which includes quotations from the third president as to his opinions of individual books and authors, and particular kinds of books, such as histories, and the evidence that this great collection included choice items from the libraries of more than half a dozen earlier colonial Americans, including William Byrd II and the founding fathers Benjamin Franklin, Richard Bland, and George Wythe.

Also available is a catalogue of German-language books, primarily theological, sent to early Georgia; the 1,200-item list of books at Whitefield's Bethesda Orphanage; and the De Brahm declarations about the five great libraries he knew in Georgia. Henry M. Muhlenburg used only superlatives when in 1774 he described the personal library of the scholarly

Reverend J. J. Zubly. Earlier, in 1757, the Commons House of Assembly declared that it took fifty-six folio pages to list the books in the so-called Parson's Library in Savannah, apparently a semi-public collection that was housed with the Anglican rector. The number of books in this collection may be suggested by the fact that listing the Bethesda items took up only twenty-three folio pages. And there are catalogues of the parochial and provincial and laymen's libraries that were sent to the southern colonies by Dr. Bray near the beginning of the eighteenth century. There are also fragmentary surviving libraries from the period, such as Dr. Bray's Annopolitan, now at St. John's College in Annapolis; the Landon Carter titles, still in his mansion of Sabine Hall; the books of James Hasell, now at the University of North Carolina at Chapel Hill; and the Jerdone family items at the College of William and Mary.

W. J. Cash, completing his *Mind of the South* at the end of the Great Depression, saw a continuity in the qualities of the region's mental character from his own time back to 1800. He was primarily concerned with the anti-intellectual aspects of that mind. In the index to his famous book the words "book" and "library" and "reading" fail to appear. In the same year as Cash's study another appeared on the earlier southern mind—a book, among historians at least, as influential and utterly different in theme and tone, for Louis B. Wright's *First Gentlemen of Virginia: Intellectual Qualities of the Early Colonial Ruling Class* is concerned almost entirely with the actual volumes southerners owned and read. It is based largely on printed book inventories Wright found in the Virginia historical journals. Its chapters focus on the great families that developed in the late seventeenth and early eighteenth centuries and on what they read as suggestions of the nature and quality of the leadership they were to exercise in the Revolutionary period. Wright identifies and characterizes their books from the short-title inventories. Though he was not sure that the Lees or Byrds or Fitzhughs read everything they owned, he offers strong evidence, from letters and diaries and published pamphlets, that they read a great deal. He points out that this aristocracy of which he writes was self-made and that the society of which it was a part was fluid; and he is aware that there is plenty of evidence that the lower or middle classes from which they rose, including yeoman farmers and indentured servants, were also readers and gatherers of books, especially the poorer clergy and schoolmasters, of which more later.

In my *Intellectual Life in Jefferson's Virginia, 1790–1830* (1964) the libraries of many more Virginians, sometimes the sons or descendants of those noted by Wright, have been analyzed. These later libraries, most of them begun by the time of the Revolution, are larger and more diversified than the colonial collections, and there is abundant evidence that these people and the holders of smaller collections were avid readers who commented on and used what they read in their own thinking and expression. Not only Jefferson, who bridges the colonial and national periods, but James Madison and John Randolph of Roanoke and William Short gathered distinguished collections and employed them profitably. And Presbyterian clergy such as John Holt Rice, scientific farmers such as John Taylor of Caroline, and lawyers such as Hugh Blair Grigsby indicate this continuity of reading and collecting books at least to the Civil War.

These studies are thus primarily of books owned by an elite of one colony-state and the use that elite made of its reading. Most of the investigation of books and reading for the other four original southern states has been more broadly based; that is, attempts have been made to consider all social and occupational classes of readers. So far, almost all of these studies have been confined to the colonial period, or perhaps to 1800, and frequently with the inference that research should proceed into the nineteenth century. Occasionally these investigators reproduce hitherto unknown inventories, but most of their effort has been to analyze the volumes according to their number, monetary value, content, and occupation of the owners. They draw some significant conclusions and infer even more. To many of these studies I am indebted, such as those of Joseph T. Wheeler for Maryland, Stephen B. Weeks for North Carolina, Walter B. Edgar for South Carolina, and Harold E. Davis for Georgia (the work of the latter two being quite recent). There are also such useful studies as those of William D. Houlette of plantation and private libraries of the Old South (1933), of Jack M. Patterson of selected private libraries of eighteenth-century Virginia (1936), of James S. Purcell of literary culture in North Carolina before 1820 (1950), and of George K. Smart of the content of Virginia private libraries from 1650 to 1787 (1938). Unfortunately, only the last has been published.

Caroline Robbins's classic *The Eighteenth-Century Commonwealthman: Studies in the Transmission, Development and Circumstance of English Liberal Thought from the Restoration of Charles II until the War with the Thirteen Colonies* (1961) has been invaluable as a guide to what one should understand of the historical, political, and social-philosophic books southern colonists owned and discussed. Almost as useful and more applicable to American-owned books is H. Trevor Colbourn's *The Lamp of Experience: Whig History and the Intellectual Origins of the American Revolution* (1965). Its usefulness is limited in its applicability to southern historical reading, however, because the author bases his conclusions regarding the sources of the region's mind on a study of a few Virginia minds and libraries (including Bland's and Jefferson's), a glance at the pamphlet warfare in Maryland between the younger Daniel Dulany and Charles Carroll of Carrollton, and a printing (almost without comment) of a few South Carolina book advertisements. In many ways more useful are a number of essays, most of them in the *William and*

Mary Quarterly, concerned with the effect of European authors on early southerners and their governmental or political philosophies. Colbourn warns that ownership did not signify reading, in contrast to Louis B. Wright's observation (well supported elsewhere) that books were too expensive to be bought merely for show. Walter B. Edgar feels that the truth lies somewhere between the two attitudes, as of course it must. But except in instances of a considerable body of books acquired by inheritance, available evidence points to extensive use of most items in libraries. The available evidence is, of course, writings such as diaries or letters or recorded conversations or legislative debates or sermons by the book owners. William Byrd II noted daily his reading in types of books in various languages and occasionally his enjoyment of a specific title. Chief Justice Trott includes in the annotations of his published and unpublished writings scores of titles of learned tomes with page and chapter.

Some comparison has been made of New England and middle colonies' libraries. Though there are a number of published inventories for the Northeast, they were peculiarly disappointing, for they do not include the complete collections of the most significant intellectual figures of the area, such as Cotton Mather or Jonathan Edwards or John Winthrop the Younger. In 1723 the first catalogue of the Harvard College Library, showing about 3,500 volumes intended primarily (almost two-thirds) for graduate students in divinity, lists what was then (and later) the largest library among eighteenth-century educational institutions. Even its proportion of theological and philosophical works was not as great as the 900 religious works out of 1,200 volumes in the Bethesda Orphanage a generation later. Apparently the College of William and Mary's library was never so preponderantly in divinity. Figures for the 1760s and 1770s show Harvard with 5,000, Yale with 4,000, William and Mary with 3,000, King's (Columbia) and Princeton and Pennsylvania and Brown and Dartmouth with

2,000 or less, with Bethesda's holdings about equal to Princeton's and ahead of Brown's and Dartmouth's—a more than creditable showing. Of the religious element in private libraries of the two regions, something will be mentioned in the appropriate chapter below.

In the middle colonies, on large farms or plantations and in the cities of New York and Philadelphia, and in smaller towns there were numerous libraries, ranging in size and subject matter over a wide spectrum. One Philadelphia bookseller in the quarter century just before the Revolution imported some £30,000 worth of books and stationery, perhaps no more in proportion to the size of the city than was sold by Robert Wells of Charleston, who claimed to have the largest stock of books in America. Edwin Wolf II's magnificent annotated *Library of James Logan of Philadelphia, 1674–1751* (1974) includes 2,185 titles in 2,651 volumes and shows that most of this great collection still exists and that, like Cotton Mather's and Thomas Jefferson's, it represents a great breadth of reading tastes, though the major emphases in each of these three great holdings is somewhat different. Benjamin Franklin's, which Manasseh Cutler viewed in 1787, probably represented even greater breadth, though there is no known listing of its estimated 4,276 volumes. Among the Pennsylvania national founding fathers, John Dickinson, James Wilson, and Benjamin Rush had respectable libraries, and Dickinson boasted about his in *Letters from an American Farmer* (1767–1768). There were also public or subscription libraries in Philadelphia, Germantown, Darby, and Lancaster. The famous and still very much alive Library Company of Philadelphia had published its first catalogue by 1733. Burlington and Trenton, in New Jersey, and New York City had similar cooperative reading institutions. Undoubtedly traces of many private collections have disappeared, though there is plenty of evidence in the records of the two middle colony metropolises of a number of small and medium-size libraries, with—certainly—a good proportion in the hands of artisans and even their apprentices. Inland New York, including the great estates of the patroons and Indian agent Sir William Johnson, had many respectable libraries. In the Pennsylvania Scotch-Irish back country too there were books, probably usually much the same in character and number as in the frontier Virginia and Carolina lands. Though there was perhaps no southern "western" town so populous or with so many educated people as Pittsburgh, perhaps Jonesboro and Knoxville in today's Tennessee had about as many Princeton-educated men by the end of the century as did the Pennsylvania outpost. In both areas there were printing presses and newspapers, and even published pamphlets or books, before 1800.

Historians never seem tired of declaring that colonial reading tastes were formed in Great Britain, or brought straight from London in a variety of ways, but this is not the exact truth. It is obvious that from Roanoke Island to the Revolution, or even to the end of the eighteenth century, English-speaking immigrants often arrived with at least the nucleus of a library—in the instances of clergy and physicians, frequently with a complete "working" collection. It is also true that from the beginning the colonists ordered books from "home" through their factors or agents, increasing the size and request as transportation became easier and more books were printed. Some settlers ordered from relatives and friends left in Europe, some through brothers or sons who had been sent to be educated in British or French schools and universities. Visits short or long to England or the Continent afforded ship captains, clergy, merchants, and affluent planters (not to mention public officials) opportunity to select for themselves. So Charles Carroll of Carrollton or Peter Manigault of Charleston or William Byrd II of Westover or Thomas Jefferson of Monticello built great collections. They were by no means alone among southern readers. But as the century progressed they added to their libraries through booksellers or merchants or itinerant salesmen such as Mason L. Weems, who sold books from Baltimore to Savannah and even a hundred or more miles inland. And they might enrich certain of their categories, such as classics or histories, by securing, as Jefferson did, choice items from the holdings of deceased neighbors and friends.

There were English or Scottish editions even of Greek and Latin classics and Hebrew religious works, or English-language translations of these, and of writings from a half dozen other languages. But by no means all the volumes in southern libraries came through English ports or had British imprints. There were Frenchmen in the southern colonies from the first generation at Jamestown, and many brought their books with them or imported them from Paris, as did the British Catholic Carrolls and many Protestants, or they bought French imprints through English and even provincial agents or booksellers. In the eighteenth century there were French-language and French-printed as well as English translations of popular books by Fénelon, Rapin, Raynal, and Voltaire. Rollin's famous histories of the ancients were often printed in French at Amsterdam. Also in the Netherlands, at The Hague, Leyden, and Amsterdam, were published scores of editions of the Latin and Greek classics, such as the famous Elzevirs beloved by Thomas Jefferson and John Randolph of Roanoke. French appears to have been read with relative ease from Maryland to Georgia, and frequently even in small libraries there were grammars and lexicons for that language. Naturally many French books were owned by Huguenots, as in Virginia and South Carolina, but perhaps more were in the libraries of British-born or -descended persons of various financial means and education.

German-language and German-printed books are not so frequent, but some may be found in every colony, especially among the Moravians and Lutherans who came south from

Pennsylvania down the trails of the piedmont and the Appalachians. Among the early Salzburger Georgians, at Ebenezer and elsewhere were whole libraries of books in German. One list appeared in 1960: as an appendix to a theological dissertation that was completed at Martin Luther University in Halle. This list of 104 titles (including a few in Latin or English), almost entirely theological, is for the most part of eighteenth-century imprints published in perhaps a dozen different German cities but largely at Halle. The library at Ebenezer supplied or lent books in Savannah and a number of communities in South Carolina. Most inventories give short titles and nothing more, but catalogues such as that of the Charleston Library Society indicate France, the Netherlands, Switzerland, Germany, Italy, and Ireland as places of imprimatur, as well as England and Scotland.

New England had published some of its own books since 1639, including the famous Bay Psalm Book of 1640 and other Puritan religious items, principally sermons and devotions, and Indian Bibles as well as governmental documents. Though Virginia and Maryland had presses near the end of the seventeenth century, only those of the latter colony survived into the eighteenth century as the second oldest permanent presses in British America. In the 1730s, South Carolina and Virginia established printing houses on a permanent basis; by mid-century North Carolina had a press; and in 1763 a printer began operations in Georgia. The press at Cambridge, Massachusetts, however, published for about two generations before the first southern colony began to print. It and other New England presses continued throughout the colonial period to pour out sermons and even (within bounds) controversial and doctrinal religious tracts, along with occasional works which may be called belletristic. Certain historians have concluded that thus was born and nurtured the intellectual independence, and a dissenting form of Calvinism, which was to shape the mind of the region and thus of America.

This is but to blow up to absurd proportion the ubiquity or

popularity of colonial New England-produced printing. The overwhelming majority of volumes, even in Puritan libraries, were printed in Great Britain, just as those were in the South. Though there is a difference in emphasis as far as proportions of theological and legal and political and belletristic writing is concerned in the two regions, the same church fathers and medieval theologians and Calvinist titles appear among the libraries of both areas. Both include Arian and Arminian and Pelagian and Calvinist and even—late in the period—pantheistic and deistic writers. Both shared with middle colonist James Logan an omnivorous taste for the classics. Examination of any one or several inventories would reveal few American-printed items. A Bay Psalm Book or two and Eliot's Indian Bibles found their way into some southern collections, and among southern Presbyterians especially there were some dozens of volumes of New England sermons, including, just before the Revolution and just after, some of the writings of Jonathan Edwards. South Carolina Calvinist Josiah Smith and Anglican Samuel Quincy delivered sermons which were first published in Boston. And several sermons and verses by Virginia Presbyterian Samuel Davies were first printed or reprinted in the northeast or middle colonies. On the other hand, southern historians such as Beverley and Smith and Lawson and Stith and Ramsay found their way into northern collections. But three of them, and most other southern writers of all complexions, were first printed in London. Incidentally, one should realize that even New England theologians usually preferred to be printed first in Britain in order to reach a larger public. Yankees and southerners alike did read many almanacs, laws, speeches, sermons, legislative minutes, manuals for tradesmen, and even volumes of verse written by their fellow colonists and printed at home, partly through the felt necessity of knowing their own situation and partly through local pride.

Perhaps the chief reading matter (other than religious) of eighteenth-century southern provincials was the newspapers published in Annapolis, Williamsburg, Charleston, New Bern, and Savannah, and later in Baltimore, Richmond, and a few other towns. The records of number of copies printed seem nowhere to exist, though a reference in the 1740s by publisher Jonas Green seems to indicate about 600 copies of his *Maryland Gazette,* and Carl Bridenbaugh suggests that perhaps, for most southern provinces from mid-century, 1,500 copies were printed. As he also suggests, this number must be multiplied several fold to reach a figure for potential or probable readers, for scores of persons may have read any single copy in the dwellings and taverns throughout each colony. In addition, there must have been hundreds more who were *read to* in public hostelries or on private estates, persons who may or may not have been literate.

A number of comments as to the contents of these (usually) weekly journals will appear in the following chapters. The papers contained much international and intercolonial and local news and an enormous amount of legislative and other official records. But they were also literary journals, presenting essays formal and familiar and borrowed from each other or from British sources, British poems, and even (occasionally) British plays. For many reasons their most interesting and significant feature for us is the considerable amount of locally composed verses and essays, including some better-than-fair verse and some really distinguished prose.

The question of percentage of literacy in the Southeast is much debated. Because of the better-organized provincial school systems of the Northeast and the early availability of locally printed material, historians once supposed that Puritan colonials especially were on the whole much more literate than southerners. There can be and has been nothing very exact on the proportion, even though several scholars have investigated it with much care. Philip A. Bruce long ago decided that he could not base an estimate of the proportion of literacy of seventeenth-century Virginians on a count or percentage of

those who signed their wills in full and those who made their
mark upon them. He preferred other documents, especially
land transfer deeds. He concluded that for its first century,
more than half of Virginia's white population was literate.
More recent historians of colonial Virginia and the rest of the
South are usually inclined to think his percentage of probable
literacy too low, and certainly too low for the eighteenth
century. D. D. Wallace, the major modern historian of South
Carolina, acknowledged a high degree of illiteracy in the white
population of the up-country in the early nineteenth century
because, he felt, the frontier had stretched the lines of communication so thin and the withering influence of the slave
economy on poor whites was so great that there was steady
deterioration of reading skill, to be improved only later. But
for the eighteenth century in Charleston and Saluda and
Enoree, judging by signed land petitions and other documents,
he found that almost everyone could read: 80 of 88, 109 of 113
and, at worst, 40 of 56 signers of various papers. Quite recently
Harold E. Davis pointed out that the literacy in early Georgia
can only be guessed, but he believes that it was rather high; for
example, from the beginning almost all the Germans could
read. And he feels with De Brahm (of whom more later) that
many or most homes contained books and readers. For South
Carolina, Wallace found only *very* rarely an illiterate public
official or church warden, even in the back country, and Bruce
found no case of an illiterate public official in Virginia among
thousands of documents in the Public Record Office.

An intriguing but highly controversial study with a mislead-
ing title, Kenneth A. Lockridge's *Literacy in Colonial New
England: An Inquiry into the Social Context of Literacy in the
Early Modern West* (1974), attempts to compare degrees of
illiteracy in New England with those of Pennsylvania and
Virginia (the latter as representative of the middle and southern provinces). The author declares that New England experienced several generations of mass illiteracy before achieving

almost universal male literacy toward the end of the colonial period. He also declares that New England's literacy was much the same as in the rest of America until the last two-thirds of the eighteenth century. He admits that his results are biased by being based largely on signatures of wills, but he defends the procedure. And he makes the interesting observation that for more than a century only a tiny proportion of Puritan congregations understood what their clergy were talking about in the sermons that are so highly touted by Perry Miller and a dozen other of our twentieth-century historians. On what seem extremely tenuous grounds (I have discussed this matter in dealing with southern colonial education elsewhere), Lockridge concludes that in Pennsylvania and Virginia literacy was in the latter eighteenth century "stagnant, albeit at a respectable level"—the same pattern that prevailed in England at the time. These and my own investigations suggest, then, a fairly high rate of literacy in the eighteenth-century South, a literacy by no means confined to the professional and large planter groups or classes.

Investigators of colonial libraries have invented fairly arbitrary but necessary classifications of books in order to determine tastes and influences. Smart's study of private Virginia libraries employs seven categories: philosophy and law, science and practical arts, classics and languages, history and biography and travel, religion, English literature, and "unclassifiable." Wheeler adapts Smart's classifications for Maryland. Edgar's studies of South Carolina collections expands and realigns Smart's into history, medicine and science, religion and philosophy, classics, magazines, literature, legal and political, geography and travel, and practical. These and other modes of classification point up characteristic facets of the colonial mind. All of them cannot be discussed here, but most of the books on the southern shelf (with one major exception) are at least represented in three categories that are considered successively in the following chapters.

The major class of books that is omitted, the medical and scientific, is a huge but generally specialized category that is represented on most southern bookshelves (other than physicians') through at least the Revolutionary period by a few herbal and gardening manuals and home medical manuals and, in the larger libraries, by the works of Newton and Boyle and some speculative astronomers. Perhaps surprisingly, there are few books on large-scale agriculture before 1789. The collections of the scholarly physicians, such as Alexander Garden and Thomas Dale of South Carolina and John Mitchell of Virginia, like those of public officials such as the second John Clayton or of clergy such as John Banister, included books and pamphlets on botany, zoology, meteorology, and geology. And the even larger libraries of Mercer and Byrd and Jefferson contained even more scientific tomes, including the *Philosophical Transactions* of the Royal Society. The average literate southern colonial was indeed aware of the plants and animals and topography of his world, but he owned relatively few books on these subjects, at least before the adoption of the Constitution.

Also necessarily omitted from this survey are the books on the fine arts, especially on architecture and music, which are again infrequent in smaller libraries but are found in all the southern provinces throughout the century. Reference books and school texts are considered only as adjuncts to the major forms.

The three categories of books here examined were represented on the bookshelves in every colony, though their number and precise nature or philosophical bias certainly change as the century develops. The first group, which combines at least two of the classifications usually suggested, considers history, law, and politics together, for each of these elements depended on the two others, in the mind of that century, even more than it does today. The second group, the religious and theological, is perhaps the most obviously distinct of the intellectual interests, but like the other two it overlaps or at times merges into one or both of the other categories. Certainly religious attitudes or theories of ecclesiastical powers crept into politics and were always present in civil law and history. And certainly theology colors or flavors the verse and essay and even the drama of the third category. The third major division, belles lettres, even though perhaps progressively more secular in theme and subject, can hardly be clearly separated from either of the two preceding classifications. The structural forms of the familiar essay and Hudibrastic verse carry political arguments, a play by Addison was the most read and best-remembered political tract of the century in the South, and hymnals or psalters were the volumes of verse most frequently found on southern shelves.

Purpose in reading is suggested by these more or less arbitrary classifications, but the southern colonist often—and obligingly for posterity—stated why he read what he did. Some specific declarations regarding his reasons for reading and owning this and that book will be quoted in the three chapters below. But books, as almost everything else in the eighteenth century, were assigned a value in terms of *usefulness*. Religious, recreational, and historical-legal-political volumes could be and were *useful*—however, in the eighteenth-century sense of the word, a fact which Thomas Jefferson suggested many times. That "everything that brought men virtue and happiness was useful" perhaps sums up the attitude. Even sober Chief Justice Nicholas Trott would have agreed that mental diversion in recreation, spiritual counseling from the church fathers and devotional manuals, and Roman and Hebrew history and law were all useful to his fellow Carolinians. Books tested by time were useful, but, like their English contemporaries, colonists preferred the classics, as well as Machiavelli and Harrington and Richard Hooker, and even Locke, in new editions which often included recent commentary; at the same time they ordered books directly from Britain or through their local booksellers within a few months of their first appearance. One planter asked for a volume of Rushworth's *Collections* on political and governmental history before it was published in Britain. That Addison's *Cato* and *Spectator* were most popular reading throughout the century in these colonies agrees perfectly with the continuing taste for them in Great Britain. Scores of books found their way into southern libraries within a few months, or at most a year or two, of their first printing in Britain. Edward Young, James Thomson, and Alexander Pope as poets and Fielding and Sterne and Smollett and a host of lesser fictionists were available in Charleston and Williamsburg almost as soon as they were in London—and, some scholars speculate, even before they were known in rural Great Britain. In other words (I have gone into this elsewhere), the so-called cultural lag simply did not exist in the eighteenth-century southern colonies and states.

Contemporary southern colonial opinion on the degree or prevalence of reading and its value is varied, but it hardly agrees with the estimates of Henry Adams and some later historians. John Pory had written as early as the 1620s that in the "southern paradise" one found a good book the choicest company. A quarter of a century later, however, one colonist found that company fatal, even while enjoying it. Bruce cites a Lower Norfolk County Virginia record of one Jacob Bradshaw, who in 1647 "received his death at the hands of God by lightening and thunder from Heaven, as he was lyinge on a chest and readinge in a Booke" (I, 404). But there was no known burning of libraries as a result of this unfortunate incident. As early as 1684 the first Virginia John Clayton, Oxford educated in theology and medicine and a scientist of some repute, observed to a physician in England that "they have few schollars so that evry one studys to be halfe Physitian half

lawyer & with a naturall accutenesse would amuse thee for
want of bookes they read men the more." But in the same letter
he begs to be sent an account of all new books and experiments, even a recipe for making a good Cheshire cheese. Forty
years later Hugh Jones, another Oxonian who spent his long
life in the two Chesapeake colonies, observed in *The Present
State of Virginia from Whence Is Inferred a Short View of
Maryland and North Carolina* (1724) that southern colonists
"were more inclinable to read men by business and conversa-
tion, than to dive into books" because they "are generally
diverted by business or inclination from profound study, and
prying into the depths of things"—at best a half-truth from a
man who communed daily with his books. Stephen Bordley of
Maryland in 1739 and 1740 repeatedly, in his letters to friends
and relatives, urged general habits of reading and the careful
perusal, for both study and enjoyment, of authors he knew in
recent editions. Maryland schoolboy Charles Carroll of Carrollton, then studying in France, found his "almost only
amusement" was reading, from poetry to history. A little later,
in America in 1772, he declared that "money cannot be laid out
better, in my opinion than in the purchase of valuable books."
The most prolific southern writer of the Revolutionary period,
crusty Landon Carter of Virginia, notes again and again in his
Diary (1965) the necessity for books and his "[over]intense
reading and observing upon all things." As did many another
southern agrarian before and after his time, Carter felt in 1777
"Nunquam minus Solus, quam cum solus" ("Never less alone
than when by myself"), the clue to the rural man's delight in
books which students of urban culture have too often failed to
appreciate. Six years before Carter expressed himself on this
greatest solace of the solitary, the generation-younger Thomas
Jefferson had written (in 1771) the first of his lifelong testimonials to the value of books, a letter to a friend suggesting a
balanced content for a beginning library, a balance achieved
by adding a dozen volumes in natural history and philosophy

to the three categories (with his own subdivisions) observed in the chapters below. By the end of the eighteenth century the Duc de La Rochefoucald-Liancourt observed in his *Travels through the United States of America* (1789) that "the tastes for reading is commoner [in Virginia] among men of the first class than in any other part of America." Jackson T. Main, in his *Social Structure of Revolutionary America* (1965), does not agree with the Frenchman's further observation that the common people of Virginia were more ignorant than elsewhere, for he finds that in Virginia, even on the western frontier, a suprisingly large number of books were shown in inventories.

These testimonials are of course predominantly of the prevalence of reading tastes among the upper and middle classes of planter and professional men—though, even so, they contradict or in part qualify claims that the New England hierarchy of clergy and its political allies constituted most of the intellectual element of colonial America. Jefferson in his plans for a public library in his native commonwealth makes it clear, as one might expect, that his recommendations for reading and books applied to all levels of the free population capable of profiting by them. The observation of German-born southern colonist William Gerard De Brahm also seems to include many social classes of southerners, and to suggest that books were one of the ladders by which settlers might rise in the New World. In his comprehensive *Report of the General Survey in the Southern District of North America* the then surveyor general of Georgia, a highly educated linguist, experimental scientist, cartographer, and military engineer, in mid-eighteenth century worked in coastal South Carolina and Georgia and as far inland as Fort Loudoun in today's Tennessee, and later turned south to East Florida. So he continued for two decades and a half, after which, as a loyalist, he resided for some years in Britain. His description (c. 1760?) of Georgia and Savannah includes some significant generalizations about the inhabitants of all the lower South:

The Author has made a general Observation among all Natives [i.e., permanent settlers] in America; they are in general of very elevated Spirits, and most of them with very little Education; yea some by reading good Authors only, acquire real Knowledge and great Wisdom. . . . He was often surprised at the good Judgments and Argumentations of Men whom he knew had been brought up intirely to Mechanism without any more Education, than reading and writing, they, after acquiring Estates, being in easy Circumstances of Life, and in a Country not as yet debauched by European Luxuries, such as Balls, Masquerades, Operas, Plays, etc., they applied themselves to reading good Authors, of which (yea the best) America has no reason to complain of a Want. There is scarcely a House in the Cities, Towns, or Plantations, but which have some Choice Authors, if not Libraries of Religious, Phylosopical, and Political Writers. Booksellers endeavor to import the newest editions, and take care to commission the best, well knowing they will not incumber their Shops long, but soon find Admirers and Purchasers; besides that, many of their books they write for are commissioned by the inhabitants.

Though Georgia was but thirty years settled, he avers, it contained at least five major (public or semi-public) libraries, three of them in Savannah, including (all together) books in thirteen languages, which he lists. This was an overly sanguine picture of widespread intellectual curiosity but it was not exaggerated in noting the education-by-reading De Brahm daily observed. And one should remember Muhlenberg's encomiums about at least one additional collection, the private library of J. J. Zubly.

In the following chapters pertinent contemporary colonial comments about each of the three areas of interest will be noted, along with eighteenth-century comments on Greek and Roman classics, which here, for the sake of space and convenience and content, are considered with more recent materials on politics and law and history, religion, and belles lettres.

Though even before the Revolution, and certainly in the last decade or so of the century, outspoken expressions against the learning of Greek and Latin by the run-of-the-mill secondary school student (Thomas Jefferson and James Maury and Jonathan Boucher were among those who *at times* spoke out against the usefulness of the classics), overwhelmingly, southern colonial and early national education was classically based, and not superficially so, as twentieth-century observers or scholars, from the Nashville Fugitives and Richard M. Gummere and Edgar Knight to Meyer Reinhold (ed., *The Classick Pages: Colonial Reading of Eighteenth-Century Americans* [1975]) and John W. Eadie (ed., *Classical Traditions in Early America* [1976]) and Leo M. Kaiser (on Landon Carter as Latinist [*Virginia Magazine of History and Biography*, 1977]) have sufficiently demonstrated. Southern colonial literates had greater depth in Greek and especially Latin authors than the elementary grammars could give them.

Though the colonial bookshelf may have been primarily pious or otherwise purposeful, one of the last eighteenth-century southern comments on reading stresses only the intellectual or philosophic pleasure it affords. On the title page of the 1798 catalogue of a private circulating library company in Baltimore was an apt quotation from one of the region's favorite books throughout the century, Fénelon's *Telemachus,* in an English translation:

Happy are they, whose amusement is knowledge, and whose supreme delight the cultivation of the mind! Wherever they shall be driven by the persecution of fortune, the means of enjoyment are still with them; and that weary listlessness, which renders life insupportable to the voluptuous and the lazy, is unknown to those, who can employ themselves in reading.

ONE

History, Politics, and Law

THOUGH RELIGIOUS WORKS WERE ALMOST SURELY THROUGHOUT the eighteenth century (as in the seventeenth) the most widely read books in the southern library, there is evidence that the three related areas of law, politics, and history were a strong second. The southern colonial bookshelf, though at times it had only ten volumes or less, was likely to carry—along with the Bible and New Testament and Book of Common Prayer or Westminster Confession and *The Whole Duty of Man*—one or more legal or historical titles. In Maryland in 1770, one poor man's three books included Rapin's *History of England* (volume 1). Other small collections included a layman's legal manual, such as as *The Compleat Lawyer* or *The Compleat Attorney* or *The Young Secretary's Guide,* or a volume or two of British or provincial statutes. On the shelf of any planter or merchant who was a local magistrate was at least one of the several convenient British compendiums for justices of the peace. One eighteenth-century southern colonial declared that, in his province of Virginia, John Mercer's *Abridgment of All the Public Acts of Assembly* (1737) was to be found in libraries even more frequently than the Bible. Another Scottish-born Virginian declared that in his county a religious topic, if brought up in a large assembly, met with dead silence, "but bring any subject from Mercer's abridgement and the youngest in Company will immediately tell you how far a grin is actionable." A volume of political philosophy, frequently Whiggish or capable of being so interpreted, less often Locke

than some others, might appear in a shelf of fewer than ten or
twenty volumes. Any southern newspaper advertisement of
books for sale, from Maryland in 1730 to Georgia in 1790, was
sure to include an impressive proportion of historical and
political and legal material, by no means all of it aimed at
professional lawyers or public officials or wealthy planters.

There is a long and fairly complex background for all this
interest. From the first landings at Roanoke Island or Jamestown, every settler was conscious that he was making history.
Sir Walter Raleigh's *History of the World* (1614) was read in
the southern provinces during all the seventeenth century and
was still being bought (usually in new editions) through the
1790s. It is concerned, of course, with the ancient world, but
along with actual classical histories (to be noted here) it afforded the Anglo-American food for thought and comparison,
along with moral teaching. Almost as popular in New England as in the Southeast, Raleigh's great compendium was read
in both areas for these and for different reasons. The same
might be said of Hooker's *Laws of Ecclesiastical Polity*
(1594–1597), which was read in early Massachusetts as well as
the Chesapeake and Carolina country, even though it justified
the Anglican position in church government. All this material
was purposeful in both the narrow modern and broader
eighteenth-century senses, for it offered practical guidance as
well as intellectual or even aesthetic satisfaction. Tastes
changed and new books, developing older doctrines or theories
or explaining new ones, appeared in ever increasing numbers
throughout the eighteenth century. But even in the final decade
after the adoption of the Constitution, the southern library
continued to have a large proportion of volumes on law,
history, and politics.

Though Henry Adams disparagingly declared that Virginians (and other southerners) by 1800 were exercising their
minds only in law, politics, and agriculture, he was perhaps
only half-consciously suggesting a truth, that eighteenth-cen-

tury southern interests were primarily or basically secular, as
opposed to or contrasted with New England's. Actually, creative thinking and expression on agriculture was almost entirely confined to the nineteenth century, beginning with John
Taylor of Caroline and Edmund Ruffin and John Beale Bordley and certain Carolinians. But law and politics, combined
with history, were a major southern interest, partly from necessity and partly from pleasure in contemplation. The middle
and northeastern libraries contain in general, though in lesser
proportion, the same books on these subjects as do the southern, and colonials to the north had largely the same motives as
their southern neighbors for owning them.

All fairly well educated Anglo-Americans knew of the reasons advanced by classical historians and political theorists for
pondering the past. Stephen Bordley of Maryland in 1739 recommended, above all authors, Cicero and then Polybius, and
in 1800 Thomas Jefferson declared that Tacitus was "the first
writer in the world." They and their contemporaries quoted
these and other ancients on the uses of a knowledge of things
that had gone before. These colonials paraphrased Graeco-
Roman authorities and contemporary British writers, and
added their own reasons for studying the record of man's
individual and societal behavior. Stephen Bordley, the Annapolis lawyer, advised his friend Matthias Harris:

The best way that I know of to avoid those Fatal consequences which
you suppose may Result from Errors in Opinion on ye Subject of
Government, is first to get well grounded in ye Original End & design
of Government in General, by reading the best Historians and other
books which treat on the Constitution of our mother Country on
which We so much depend, and next to Consider what Arts or Steps
have been regularly taken among ourselves toward making a difference between the English Constitution & our own here, & what not; &
when all this is done, a man ought to be well aware of Byasses from
Interest Passion friendship Authority or any other motive but ye pur
dictates of Right Reason.

Bordley made several sententious but significant comments

to Harris and to his own younger brother on methods of learning history, and of his personal reaction to reading Rapin's and Rollin's works and some quite different chronicles. His fellow Marylanders, such as the Carrolls, both Roman Catholic and Protestant branches of that family, were as concerned with reading as he. One barrister Protestant Carroll, educated in Britain, asked his London agent to keep him supplied (in 1764) with every political pamphlet he could find, as well as numerous Whiggish or Whiggishly inclined histories. His Roman Catholic cousin, Charles Carroll of Carrollton, French and English educated, later signer of the Declaration, an avid book collector of even the principal deistic and atheistic writers of his time and also of Whiggish historians, early in his life (1759) received from his father the planter, Charles of Doughregan Manor, a significant bit of advice representing upper-class attitudes toward legal knowledge:

It is a shame for a gentleman to be ignorant of the laws of his country and to be dependent on every dirty pettifogger. . . . On the other hand, how commendable it is for a gentleman of independent fortune not only [not] to stand in need of mercenary advisers, but to be able to advise his friends, relations, and neighbors of all sorts. . . . Suppos you will be called on to act in any public character, what an awkward figure you would make without knowledge of the law either as a legislator, judge, or even an arbiter of differences among your neighbors and friends. Apply as if your whole and sole dependence was to be on the knowledge of the law.

The younger Carroll, then studying at the London Inns of Court, may not have needed this advice. But across the Potomac in Virginia a decade later, planter Landon Carter, probably the most prolific pamphleteer of his colony in the pre-Revolutionary period, addressed his less intellectual son, Robert Wormeley Carter, in similar vein in a note inscribed in a copy of *The Acts of Assembly, now in force, in the Colony of Virginia* (1769): "This volume contains the Laws of your Country, and as no Gentleman should be ignorant of them I am persuaded I shall not stand in need of any arguments to enforce my desire to you." The elder man warned that the study of such statutes might at first prove dull and insipid but that it would produce an informed citizen capable of judging the values of these and other laws, and even of advising friends concerning possible legislative action.

Almost twenty years later, Jefferson wrote to his future son-in-law Thomas Mann Randolph: "I have proposed to you to carry on the study of law, with that of Politics & History. Every political measure will for ever have an intimate connection with the laws of the land; and he who knows nothing of those will always be perplexed & often foiled by adversaries having the advantage of that knowledge over him." Jefferson's neighbor, Dr. George Gilmer, possessor of a wide-ranging and thoughtful mind and a well-stocked library, pondered and interpreted the meaning of the Revolution in his commonplace book in terms of politics and history. He quoted from David Hume's *Essays*: "Mankind are so much the same in all times and places that history informs us of nothing new or strong in this particular. Its chief use is only to discover in all varieties of circumstances and situations, and furnishing us with materials from which we may form our observations and become acquainted with the regular springs of human action and behavior."

These men and their contemporary colonists had often read and frequently referred to well-known theories as to the uses of history in politics and the possible methods of studying both. Principally, they refer for theory to the classical historians or to English and (more rarely) French eighteenth-century thinkers, all represented on their shelves. The republican or radical British Whigs of the later seventeenth century and their heirs of the earlier eighteenth, the moderate Whigs and the moderate conservatives of integrity, such as Bolingbroke, as well as the later conservatives of the Hume-Burke variety, were among those whom these colonials pondered but whose advice they did not necessarily follow. Most early Americans shared with

many of these writers the cyclical theory of history, which
involves that discipline fundamentally with politics and law:
that what has happened will or may happen again. Thus one
pseudonymous southern essayist in the *Maryland Gazette* in
1745 produced with this sort of reading in his background
perhaps the most thoughtful comment of the American eighteenth century upon the uses of history.

Caroline Robbins in *The Eighteenth-Century Commonwealthman* and her many discerning studies of individual
writers, Richard B. Morris and his group's evaluations of
colonial Americans and law, and Trevor Colbourn in *The
Lamp of Experience: Whig History and the Intellectual Origins of the American Revolution* examine in detail (albeit
uneven detail) Anglo-American and American knowledge and
employment of Old World ideas. All insist, and rightly, that no
book or group of books incited men to revolt. Most of these
historians (including some not named here for lack of space)
have concluded that what occurred was a conservative revolution. Howard Mumford Jones calls the creation of the New
World republic the last great triumph of the Enlightenment,
and of course he does not attribute that creation to particular
European books or philosophers. Bernard Bailyn, in his
Pamphlets of the American Revolution and elsewhere, holds to
his "old-fashioned view" that independence was the result of
an ideological movement, a movement only in part inspired by
Old World political theory. In all this is the implicit or sometimes expressed assumption that colonial law, history, and
politics differ little in the three major groups of colonies.
Though the presence of slavery has always been felt and noted,
its apparent failure to affect southern libertarian action, appre-
ciably or negatively, has never been satisfactorily explained,
though Edmund Morgan recently made a magnificent effort to
do so.

Colbourn devotes a chapter to Jefferson and has little else to
say of other southern owners of politically slanted books,

though he borrows his title from Patrick Henry, and, as previously noted, Richard Bland, Daniel Dulany, Jr., and Charles Carroll of Carrollton receive some attention. Madison is barely mentioned. The rest of the founding fathers from south of the Susquehannah are ignored, though a few names are recorded in passing. It is not our intention to claim that southern intellectual interests were drastically different from those of the colonists to the north, or that southern intellectuals were true liberals in any twentieth-century sense, or that widely read southern revolutionists were the only begetters of the Republic. But a look at southern reading in matters related to government and society may offer some indication as to why they supplied leaders, and perhaps the greatest proportion of major leaders, in the creation of the United States.

Books on law appeared on southern shelves long before the eighteenth century. Under the Virginia Company before 1624, books at Jamestown include volumes of English statutes and Sir William Stanford's *Les Plees del Coron* [*The Pleas of the Crown* (first ed. 1557)]—the latter title owned by Jefferson in a 1583 edition in the early nineteenth century and by many others between. More popular from its first publication in 1678 was Sir Matthew Hale's *Pleas of the Crown* (in Latin or English) and, later in 1716, William Hawkins's *A Treatise of Pleas of the Crown*. These books were almost indispensable for colonial courts or legislative assemblies and practicing lawyers, but like most other collections-with-commentary of legal practice, they were also found in the libraries of planters, physicians, and clergy.

In the older southern colonies the printed laws of the particular provinces, complete or abridged, were the most popular legal items *recorded* in library inventories. Mercer's *Abridgment* and its local popularity have been noted, but somewhat more remarkable is the frequent presence of certain expensive volumes such as Thomas Bacon's *Laws of Maryland at Large* (Annapolis, 1765) and Nicholas Trott's *The Laws of the Prov-*

ince of South Carolina (Charleston, 1736). There were also many lesser editions for individual colonies, and widely distributed to members of provincial legislatures and county commissions of the peace were the official periodic compilations published by the authorized printers in the various capitals. The most popular legal title in South Carolina, next to Trott's *Laws,* was British Thomas Wood's *Institute of the Laws of England,* and it is frequently on the shelves of Chesapeake colonials. Useful to layman as well as lawyer were Giles Jacob's *A New Law Dictionary* (1729) and Henry Swinburne's ubiquitous ecclesiastical law volume, *A Briefe Treatise of Testaments and Last Wills* (1590, and eight other editions by 1743, with another in 1803), the latter almost always listed as "Swinburn on wills." Sir Edward Coke's *Reports and Institutes of the Laws of England,* in many editions, was in the larger libraries from the seventeenth century. Jefferson, who owned several volumes of the great works, in his college days referred to Coke as "an old dull scoundrel," but many years later praised the *Institutes* as "executed with so much learning and judgement that I do not recollect that a single position in it has ever been judicially denied." In the colonies, where parents too often died young, John Godolphin's *The Orphan's Legacy* (1674) was most useful, as was Swinburne's work (classed as ecclesiastical law), for the matters of the wills and legacies and duties of execution here discussed were functions in Britain of the ecclesiastical courts.

Lawyers had to afford these books and others felt they had to. In every parish vestries were concerned with children left with guardians or with guardians who failed in their duties. Professional men, seamen, merchants, and planters, great and small, were vitally concerned with land, and this meant litigation, as well as the recording and conveyance of deeds.

Everywhere in the South, as in rural England and to some extent in the northern colonies, one of the first duties of a man who held property was to serve as a justice on a county commission of the peace. As noted, even in the seventeenth century few if any colonial justices were illiterate (there are indications that in the eighteenth century a scattered few, serving along the extended frontier, may not have been able to read and write). The first public office held by almost every legislative and judicial and even military leader in the century of the Revolution was on the commission of the peace, though family founder William Fitzhugh was a member of the Virginia House of Burgesses before he became (in 1684) a Stafford County justice. He lived in a frontier county on guard against Indian depredations, but there is every indication that his fellow justices were, as he was, far more than merely literate. Though he was a practicing barrister as well as a large landowner, the other members of his commission, as far as is now evident, had no formal legal training. Actually most county commissions of the peace were made up of landowners, and occasionally merchants, whose knowledge of judicial matters came from volumes of statutes and procedures such as those just mentioned, from experience in the "lesser" cases, such as their courts handled, but most specifically from one or more of the remarkable manuals designed for the guidance of amateur *and* professional jurists in rural England and in the colonies. Jefferson owned, and apparently used, several of these guides, as did the learned South Carolina Chief Justice Trott two generations earlier, and all sorts of people who did not serve in judicial capacities. At county seats were frequently collections of these and other legal works, designed for the particular use of the justices but in fact borrowed and read by many other persons and paid for through the county levy.

Jefferson's manuals included two seventeenth-century and three eighteenth-century British aids to justices of the peace, and two Virginia-published and -authored eighteenth-century similar works. George Webb, a justice of the peace in New Kent County, had printed at Williamsburg in 1736 *The Office and Duty of a Justice of the Peace . . . Collected from the*

*Common and Statute Laws of England, and Acts of Assembly,
now in force; and adapted to the Constitution and Practice of
Virginia,* one of the earliest of its kind produced in the colonies. Along with it, Jefferson had William Waller Hening's *The
New Virginia Justice, comprising the Office and Authority
of a Justice of the Peace, in the Commonwealth of Virginia*
(1795), by the later compiler of the famous *Statutes at Large of
Virginia.* There was, in addition, attorney Richard Starke's
Office and Authority of a Justice of the Peace (1774), by a
Virginian of legislative and magisterial experience. In Charles-
ton an assistant judge of the court of general sessions, William
Simpson, in 1761 published *The Practical Justice of the
Peace and Parish-Officer of . . . South Carolina,* a best seller in
that colony from the time it appeared.

British manuals much used by southern settlers included
Michael Dalton's (1618), Sir Richard Bolton's (1638), Joseph
Keble's (1689), William Nelson's (1710), Joseph Shaw's (1728),
and Richard Burn's (1755), all of which continued to appear in
new editions that were sold in the colonies up to and during
the Revolution and referred to long after that time. Of these,
the manual most frequently present from Maryland through
Georgia was Dalton's *The Countrey Justice; containing the
practice of the Justices of the Peace as well in as out of their
Sessions.* In rural Britain and America, magistrates found this
earliest handbook of its kind a prized resource. Aphra Behn,
the seventeenth-century English dramatist, in her perhaps
satiric and at least facetious play *The Widow Ranter, or, The
History of Bacon in Virginia* (composed c. 1688), jibes at New
World uncouthness, especially in her court scenes depicting
provincial jurists as dependent on Dalton without being able
to read him. As in another work of hers, *Oroonoko,* roguish and
boorish colonial officials are the butt of her ridicule, and she
has one magistrate say to another: "Why Brother though I
can't read my self, I have had Dalton's Country Justice read
over to me two or three times, and understand the Law"

(*Works*, ed. Montague Summers; 5 vols., London [1915], 4:264
[act 3, sc. 1]). The allusion applies as much to British rural
illiteracy as to southern colonial but perhaps is indebted most
to the comic Shakespearean constable–country magistrate tradition. Though as a scholar has shown recently, the idea of
American illiteracy she may have inferred from the historical
report-documents employed as her source.

Emphasis in Dalton is on the English common law and the
statutes in some of the collections noted above as widely held
in the southern colonies. One can be more than reasonably
sure that every southern colonial legislator and judge, every
administrative official, every professional lawyer, every land-
holder of at least several acres, and every justice of the peace
and vestrymen owned or had available Dalton's *Countrey
Justice.* The colonial period, one repeats, was a litigious age,
in which royal governors seem to challenge or to tax or to
usurp the colonist's right to land, or the conveyance of title to
various sorts of property (including exports and imports), or
certain aspects of personal liberty. Lesser and petty crimes had
to be considered by lay judges in thinly populated areas.
Everyone who could read turned to Dalton and the provincial
or English statutes to find out whether he was receiving or how
he was administering justice. Colonial assemblymen were
arguing legal right, personal and political, from their first 1619
session at Jamestown straight through and beyond the 1788
constitutional debates. Whenever they spoke or wrote, they
buttressed their arguments in the New World situation with
references to printed laws and legal commentaries.

Almost surely among the books John White lost at Roanoke
Island were some histories of the ancients and of the British
peoples. Certainly from early Jamestown there were copies of
Greek and Roman and British chronicles and biographies.

Internal evidence in the Virginia-composed first New World writings (1608, 1609?) of John Smith, William Strachey's *Historie of Travell into Virginia Britania* (1612), and George Sandys's *Ovid's Metamorphosis* (1626) suggests that these colonists had classical histories and sixteenth-century British annals (among other books) with them in the "rudeness" of America. William Camden's *Britannia* (1586 in Latin, 1610 in English) and Sir Richard Baker's *Chronicle of the Kings of England* (1641, 1643) were in several colonies during the seventeenth century and continued in popularity all through the eighteenth. Alongside them, but covering only some centuries of the ancient world, was the already noted enormously popular, indeed ubiquitous, Sir Walter Raleigh's *History of the World* (1614 and dozens of later editions) and Plutarch's *Lives of the Noble Grecians and Romans* in North's sixteenth-century, Dryden's seventeenth-, and the Langhornes' eighteenth-century translations or in Latin-Greek versions (several of the last were owned by Jefferson). Some editions of two later writers were offered for sale in town and country in southern states at least as late as 1797. Camden and Baker were antiquarian, detailed, and anecdotal and supplied British people with their own history in editions popular until sometime after Rapin's (French 1724, English soon after). The "incomparable Plutarch" was read for moral and historical instruction throughout the American seventeenth century, and in the eighteenth for backgrounds "for liberty in a republican garb." Raleigh offered Christian history, with divine providence as a guiding force. He warned against the false wisdom and errors of political leaders and against tyranny as the most detestable form of government. He extolled monarchy and denounced democracy as the tyranny of the multitude, and he saw history as moral instruction, to be presented in the form of pen portraits of major historical personages.

Flavius Josephus's *History* of the Jews was owned in every colony—in Greek, Latin, or English—by clergymen, physi-

cians, planters, public officials, and other folk from the latter
seventeenth century to 1798. Every man who wanted to be
intelligent about Old Testament matters felt he must have a
copy. It was the second most popular history in South Carolina. In 1709 William Byrd II read it in the Greek version
before breakfast. Jefferson owned several editions in Latin or
English. The third president also owned Polybius's *General
History,* as had other southern colonials since the 1690s at
latest. From this stiff moral history they learned how earlier
empires had risen, flourished, and declined, and inevitably
compared them with the far-flung domain of which they were a
part. Perhaps Polybius did not come into his own until the
constitutional debates of 1787–1788, but he was on the southern bookshelf long before.

Another sort of chronicle popular before 1700 was John
Rushworth's *Historical Collections of Private Passages of State*
(1680–1692), an account of parliamentary matters in the stormy
years of the Puritan revolution, and sometimes interpreted as
having a parliamentary bias. It was still a usual item in medium or large southern libraries in 1798. Edward Hyde's (earl
of Clarendon) *History of the Rebellion* (1702–1704), written in
the seventeenth century, was a Tory account of considerable
literary merit and integrity. Bishop Gilbert Burnet's *History of
the Reformation of the Church of England* (1679–1714) and
History of His Own Time (1724–1734), liberal Whiggish inter-
pretations of recent British history, were read all through the
eighteenth century in every southeastern province. They were
on Jefferson's recommended lists of historical reading. Law-
rence Echard's *Roman History* (1698/1699), largely derivative
and monarchical, was for much of the eighteenth century the
most popular account of the ancient republic, from "the Building of the City to the Perfect Settlement of the Empire by
Augustus Caesar." The same author's *History of England*
(1707–1720), from Julius Caesar to the end of the reign of
James II, is an entertaining Tory account in the Clarendonian

tradition, the most popular history of England in America until Tindall's translation of Rapin. Also of the first part of the eighteenth century is Bishop White Kennett's *Complete History of England* (1706), widely read from Maryland to Georgia. Kennett incidentally is also remembered as an original member of the S.P.G. and as compiler of the first exclusively American bibliography, *Bibliotheca Americanae Primordia: An Attempt Towards Laying the Foundation of an American Library* . . . (1713).

Thus by the beginning of the eighteenth century the southern colonial reader was familiar with dozens of histories of the ancients and of Britain, almost all of them secular and usually didactic. They were almost all also monarchical, though many of them place stress on personal liberty and, directly or indirectly, on the possible clash between governmental or crown prerogative and the liberty of the subject. Readers who were conscious of the cyclical concept were to increase in the new century, but in the story of their own country or of ancient Greece and Rome they had already noted examples of rise and decline. Translators of the historical classics and later seventeenth-century historians of contemporary Britain were influenced, sometimes almost imperceptibly, by what had just happened or was happening in England, such as the Puritan revolution and Commonwealth, the restoration of the Stuarts, the Glorious Revolution of 1689, and by the purely political writings of Hobbes and Filmer, Harrington and Sidney and Locke, who (with others) are to be noted in a moment.

The new histories of the eighteenth century were even more influenced by particular political ideologies than were the earlier accounts. At the same time they were of broader scope, for they were concerned with Carthage and Egypt as well as Greece and Rome, and with modern continental Europe as well as Great Britain. Copies of the *Universal History* (compiled by many hands, and in the first twenty volumes [1747–1755] concerned with the ancient world) were surprisingly widespread, especially considering their cost and size.

Puffendorf's *Introduction to the Principal Kingdoms and States of Europe*, though the first English version was in 1695, marked a pattern of broadening historical interests in its several eighteenth-century English and French editions.

French writers, in their own language or in English translation, were with few exceptions the most widely represented interpreters of England and even of the ancient world. Charles Rollin, Jansenist rector of the University of Paris, published his readable and instructive *Ancient History* in 1730–1738, and after his death his *Roman History* was completed by friends and brought out about 1741. Both appeared in new editions throughout the century, and an eight-volume printing of the *Ancient History* appeared in Boston as late as 1805. Both were read widely throughout our first national period. At least one of them appears in a 1767 Georgia library, in numerous pre-Revolutionary newspaper advertisements, in mid-eighteenth-century Maryland sermons and letters, in John Randolph of Roanoke's recommendations to a young relative, in John Breckinridge's books (carried to Kentucky in 1792), in the collections of individuals and groups in the Carolinas, and in 1797 in the inventory of a Lunenburg County Virginia country store. One should add that the books were favorites of John Adams and his family in Massachusetts. Though Rollin's works have been called shortcuts to the classics, they offered much more to their readers, for they proceed from the cyclical theory and they are theistic. A recent study has shown that Rollin's influence complements that of "the dissident Whig authors" who kept alive a republican ideology in Walpole's England and in his America. By 1800 the books were available in free schools and mechanics' apprentice programs, for they seemed to preach that the republican cycle in America must continue or all would be lost.

Southern colonials as well as some other Americans showed great interest in the histories of revolutions in the western world by Abbé Rene Aubert de Vertot. Though Jefferson owned a 1689 first edition of the story of the revolution in Portugal (as well as a much later English edition), his other works by this author were eighteenth-century printings. Vertot's *Revolutions of the Roman Republic* was offered for sale many times in Williamsburg between 1751 and 1772 and was owned in Charleston in 1750 and in Baltimore in 1798. The accounts of revolutions in Sweden and Spain were in libraries in Maryland, Virginia, Georgia, and South Carolina. Though the author uncritically repeated certain ancient historians, he had a talent for narrating and interpreting, with an eye on current French affairs, which contributed to the popularity of his books for a full century. He stressed love of liberty as the first motive in founding the Roman Republic and the Romans' nobility of character as long as they remained husbandmen and called "their greatest Captains from the Plough to command their Armies." These were among the reasons why he was read. Though he was not quite as popular as at least three English and another French historian, he had a considerable following in the South. See, for example, the references to him in the *Virginia Gazette Index*.

Though he came relatively late upon the eighteenth-century scene, Voltaire and his histories appear frequently in the library lists of every southern colony: his *Age of Louis XIV*, the *History of Charles XII of Sweden*, the *History of the Russian Empire*, the *General History of Europe*, and several other titles. The Anglican Reverend Thomas Cradock of Maryland, a learned litterateur, owned the 1759 edition of Voltaire's *Essay on Universal History*. John Randolph of Roanoke wrote that one of the first books he read (c. 1780–1781) was the *History of Charles XII*. Rousseau sent volumes of the same work to his friend, Dr. George Gilmer of Albemarle. Parson Weems, the itinerant bookseller extraordinary, sold hundreds of copies of Voltaire's histories in all the southeastern states in the 1790s and early 1800s. Country stores in Virginia carried Voltaire's *Works* in stock. Devout Roman Catholic Charles Carroll of Carrollton in 1771 asked to have all new Voltaire essays sent to him from France. A Maryland sheriff and Virginia and North Carolina governors, physicians, and planters owned many Voltaire titles, but his histories were most frequent. "An 'in-fidel' but a great historian," a Presbyterian scholar-cleric of 1800 insists, and he gives the *Age of Louis XIV* (1751, [English 1752]) pre-eminence as the first work to show how "intimately revolutions, and other national events are often connected with the current of literary, moral, and religious opinions; and how much a knowledge of one is frequently fitted to elucidate the other." One should remember that in *Louis XIV* Voltaire condemned the persecution of French Protestants, though he also blamed them for obstinacy in small matters. His biting comment on English dissent was allowable because he was even sharper in his allusions to Catholicism. His *Philosophical Dictionary* (1765), with its strangely anti-Christian bias, seems not to have been read much before the end of the century. All together, Voltaire's remarkable popularity in the eighteenth-century southeast may be another suggestion that that region's culture was basically secular.

Throughout the century—at least from its first appearance in English in 1725–1731—*Histoire d'Angleterre* (orig. ed. 1724), by the French Protestant and Whig Paul de Rapin-Thoyras, was the most popular account of the mother country in the southeastern colonies and states. As the Whigs had done since the late seventeenth century, and indeed as Sir Henry Spelman and others had done earlier, Rapin felt the necessity of going back to the Anglo-Saxons to explain English democratic institutions and constitutions. He traces English history from Julius Caesar and brings it through the reign of Charles I. Most southern colonials owned the English edition, improved with notes by the translator Nicholas Tindal, who later continued the story to the end of the reign of George I. Before

1732 Robert Carter of Virginia owned the combined Rapin-Tindal version in fifteen volumes, and it seems to have been the history owned by the Reverend Richard Ludlam of South Carolina by 1728. Though its ultra-Whiggish point of view cannot account for all of its popularity, the fact that colonials saw the history of the mother country through this essentially republican interpretation must have influenced their minds from the 1730s. Almost always colonial readers refer to Rapin with approval, an interesting exception being Maryland lawyer Stephen Bordley, who wrote in 1739 that since he had read the first volume of the history he thought less of the author he had known previously only by repute. Jefferson, who like William Byrd II and Dr. William Fyffe of South Carolina and others owned a French edition, told a friend as late as 1815 that "it was still the best history of England, for Hume's tory principles are . . . insupportable," and in 1825 wrote another friend that "of England there is as yet no general history so faithful as Rapin's." One should recall that among eighteenth-century histories he owned not only Hume but Whiggish Catharine Macaulay and the shorter and more recent (London, c. 1796–1801) history by John Baxter, the last of which he attempted to have reprinted in America. He also had a copy of Oliver Goldsmith's *History* (1764). But this French exposition and narrative of the prerogatives of the crown and the rights and privileges of the people, with the observation that the Saxons did not invest their kings with the power of changing laws when they pleased or of raising taxes at their pleasure, remained for Jefferson and his countrymen the most satisfactory account of their European progenitors, obviously in part because it fitted conceptions already arrived at from experience and from other political theorists. Again one must note that Rapin's popularity was not confined to the South, though Daniel Dulany, Sr., Charles Carroll of Carrollton, Richard Bland and Thomas Jefferson, Henry Laurens and John Joachim Zubly were among the Frenchman's attentive readers.

There were English historians in the eighteenth century who wrote of their own country, and several of them were relatively popular, for various reasons, in the South. Novelist Tobias Smollett's *Complete History of England, From the Descent of Julius Caesar to the Treaty of Aix la Chapelle* appeared in 1757, with a continuation in 1763–1765. Smollett's predilection for the Whig point of view wore off, he said, as he proceeded in its composition. Yet his historical work is hardly as strongly Tory as that of his fellow Scot David Hume. Smollett's work was enormously popular in America from its first appearance. The inventories indicate that southern colonials, such as D. P. Custis, bought Smollett's narrative in the year of its first appearance, and advertisements in the *Virginia* and *South Carolina* gazettes indicate that the first edition, and then the first edition with the *Continuation,* were offered in colonial bookstores within a year of their publication. The latter was still offered in a country general store in Virginia in 1797.

Another novelist, Oliver Goldsmith, was read in the South for his Greek (1774) and Roman (1768) histories—potboilers recommended to nephews by Jefferson, who suggested, especially for them, Goldsmith's slightly earlier *History of England, in a Series of Letters from a Nobleman to His Son* (1764). In 1796 traveling salesman Mason L. Weems sold seventy-five complete sets of Goldsmith's writings, including the histories, in Richmond alone. William Robertson, Scottish educator and author of such classics as the *History of the Reign of the Emperor Charles V* (1769, with a Philadelphia edition in 1770), produced two other works that were read in the eighteenth-century South, *History of Scotland* (1759) and *History of America* (1777), which are found fairly frequently in libraries from Maryland to Georgia. A robust Presbyterian Christian opposed to Whitefield and "enthusiasm" and on cordial terms with Hume and Gibbon, he was commented upon most unfavorably for his history of America by Jefferson in 1785, who called him a "compiler only of the relations of others." Not surprisingly in view of the Caledonian element in the population of the Southeast, his *History of Scotland* is found more often in southern libraries than is his *America*.

Politically the two most significant British historians of their own country during the eighteenth century, both widely read in the South, presented English history from widely differing points of view. Catharine Macaulay, ardent Whig and controversialist, who declared she had from early youth read with delight those historians "that exhibit liberty in its most exalted state," published the first volume of *The History of England from the Accession of James I to that of the Brunswick Line* in 1763. It was never completed, but nine volumes were published with additions by 1783. Her volumes were widely advertised and sold from Baltimore through Charleston, and in 1784 she visited George Washington at Mount Vernon. Jefferson had a complete first edition of the nine volumes; and long before they were completed, Whiggish Virginian James Maury ordered all volumes that had appeared through his Tory friend and fellow clergyman Jonathan Boucher, who lived at a seaport as Maury did not.

Quite different but represented by even more southern examples, perhaps because it was published earlier (in 1754–1759), was the famous history by the political conservative and religious sceptic, the Scot David Hume. His *History of England from the Invasion of Julius Caesar to the Revolution of 1688* was read by the religious orthodox and the sceptical as well as by the liberal and conservative (in varying ways) southern colonists. They were still buying this book in 1798 and into the next century. Charles Carroll of Carrollton bought the volumes as they came out. Hume's Toryism, modern scholars more or less agree, was more superficial than that of Burke or Bolingbroke. His political ideas, showing the detachment and discernment of the sceptic, have many qualities in common with those of the British liberal Whigs of his time, as do his ideas on parliament and on change of government and on

party. But he did not believe in the social contract as the basis
for liberty, that the growth of wealth and civilization endan-
gered liberty, as did those radical Whigs. He held that Americans were unconquerable and wished his government would
crush demagogues instead of trying to crush colonists. Though
the orthodox Presbyterian parson Samuel Miller in 1800,
weighing Hume's qualities as a historian, could declare that
the Scot's work deserved comparison with the best produced in
Greece and Rome, rationalist Thomas Jefferson, who may
have felt some compatibility with Hume in his religious views,
condemned the historian. Jefferson bitterly resented Hume's
popularity: "I remember well the enthusiasm with which I
devoured [the *History*] when young, and the length of time, the
research and the reflection which were necessary to eradicate
the poison it had instilled in my mind . . . it is this book which
has undermined the free principles of English government . . .
and has spread universal toryism over the land." Needless to
say, Hume's *History* is not on any of Jefferson's many lists of
recommended reading. As Douglass Adair has shown, however, James Madison probably owed some of his profoundest
insights into the dangers of faction and the advantages of large
republics to Hume's political essays, which were as well
known in America as the *History*. But there is little evidence
that Hume was a profound or (from a liberal point of view)
pernicious influence anywhere in America.

As this brief survey of library volumes on law and history may
suggest, it is doubtful that more politically minded people ever
lived among the British than the southern colonials. From the
days of the Virginia Company of London, they were always
concerned with their rights as Englishmen. The charters
granted to the Virginians under the company and then the
crown, the Proprietary Charters and Fundamental Constitu-

tions of Maryland and the Carolinas, all explicitly or implicitly reflect royal or parliamentary prerogatives in some relation to colonial rights. Incidentally, religion was never *the* primary factor in determining home government and southern colonial relationship, though it was at times a factor. But from Captain John Smith as president of the council (1607–1609), and including early governors Yeardley and Wyatt and their first General Assembly of 1619, through later legislatures and individuals from Maryland to Georgia, bitter attitudes were often expressed toward authority in Britain acting as prerogative— an authority which failed to understand colonial problems because it had not experienced them. And frequently, in more friendly tones, messages and reports were sent back to the Board of Trade and the Plantations explaining colonial needs in taxes, land policies, provincial and parish church organization, militia, and agricultural incentive, among a dozen other matters. Surviving journals of councils and houses of assembly and printed, enacted laws indicate how earnestly colonials pondered and debated these things. One should read, for example, the arguments of William Fitzhugh in the 1680s as to the necessity for the immediate validation of enacted colonial laws and the proper relationship of parliaments to superior courts, the first based on a mixture of experience and English precedent, the second ostensibly on English precedent alone. Or one should see the Virginia legislature and judicial records of a generation later, with their evidence of Sir John Randolph's learned familiarity with English parliamentary procedure. Parallel situations appear in the legislative documents of the proprietary colonies even before they were taken over (in the case of Maryland not permanently) by the crown. Many colonial governors, though they were convinced British imperialists, developed such an interest (including economic) in their provinces that they too presented arguments from the American point of view to home authorities. Viceroys and legislators were careful to cite English political and legal precedent in presenting almost any case. When the colonials finally came to protest the Stamp Act and then to state reasons for independence, their oral and written polemics were studded with references to British political writing and constitutions, as well as to general history.

Whether mid- or later eighteenth-century political arguments came basically from need and experience and were bolstered by precedents from the writers of antiquity and the Renaissance and their own time, or whether the rebellious Americans got their ideas of their rights from their libraries and reading, has long been discussed, with the frequent conclusion that local and immediate incentive came first, books second. Certainly political writing was a conscious and cited asset of the New World southern settler in expressing his strong feelings. What may be glanced at here are the principal political materials he had on his bookshelves, in addition to the already noted legal and historical volumes which were (even the classics) profoundly political in point of view.

Early in the seventeenth century some of these materials were already in the colonies. A clergyman in 1635 is the first recorded owner of a copy of Richard Hooker's *Of the Laws of Ecclesiastical Polity* (1594–1597), the classic of the English Reformation settlement and justification of the Anglican position in church government, a work often referred to in secular political pamphlets or treatises to the end of the eighteenth century. Copies were sent by the famous Dr. Bray to Maryland and South Carolina before the end of the seventeenth century, and even earlier a copy appears in the library of Governor Francis Nicholson (successively of Maryland, Virginia, and South Carolina). All through the eighteenth century—from a planter's inventory of 1701, South Carolina's Chief Justice Trott's reference in 1703, the library lists of North Carolina Governor Arthur Dobbs in 1765, and a number of libraries of clergy and planters (including Richard Bland's in 1776, Edward Lloyd's in 1796, the Library Company of Baltimore's in

1798) to Thomas Jefferson's collection—may be found Hooker's great book. Jefferson, significantly, included his 1723 edition in his classification "Politics." The sixteenth-century Florentine, Machiavelli, a prolific writer best known for *The Prince* and in our period also for *Discourses on Livy,* and recently hailed as the transmitter (through Harrington) of certain classical political ideologies, is no longer labeled the epitome of wily and unscrupulous politics, though in the nineteenth century, and often since, he has been so characterized. His opposition to mercenary armies and his belief in a native militia, for example, may have come from the Greeks and Romans, but it was carried on by Harrington and the neo-Harringtonians of the end of the seventeenth century into the eighteenth and became a familiar issue (though really a bogey) with the southern colonials, who mention it in their Revolutionary period pamphlets and long before in all their provincial newspapers. Machiavelli is referred to both favorably and unfavorably, as early as 1624, in a recently published letter from English country gentleman George Wyatt to his son, the Virginia resident, colonial governor Sir Francis. Evidently the older man thought the younger knew Machiavelli well or had this Florentine's works with him at Jamestown. Sir Francis, clearly, was to be the kind of good albeit strong magistrate recommended by Machiavelli and by the so-called Real (Radical) Whigs almost a century later. George Wyatt refers to Polybius and Machiavelli on the proper organization of a militia, with the obvious assumption that such a volunteer army will be the colony's fighting force. Like Hooker, Machiavelli stood on southern shelves throughout the eighteenth century, owned by clergymen and lawyers and planters, including at least a Maryland and a Virginia signer of the Declaration. Jefferson owned several editions, and Madison recommended in 1782 the complete *Works* as a necessity in the political section of the Library of Congress.

Other seventeenth-century or earlier political writers were

more or less well known in the colonial South throughout that century, and sometimes through the next. Francis Bacon's miscellaneous works, including his utopian *New Atlantis* (usually printed with the always popular *Sylva Sylvarum*), extended their influence and presence, not yet adequately measured, into the eighteenth century, though in the latter days it was never so popular as Sir Thomas More's *Utopia* of an earlier time, which was to be found in dozens of southern collections before 1800. James Harrington, a writer hailed by a recent historian as the only legitimate English interpreter of Machiavelli for the eighteenth century and as "the central figure among the 'classical' [i.e., Graeco-Roman] republicans," was represented on a number of shelves by *The Commonwealth of Oceana* (1656) throughout the eighteenth century. He differed from the later group of so-called neo-Harringtonians, which included Walter Moyle, John Toland, Viscount Molesworth, John Trenchard, and Thomas Gordon (also known as Real Whigs), in that he saw medieval politics as incoherent, whereas they identified the commonwealth of freeholders with the ancient (Saxon) constitution.

Besides certain later seventeenth-century libertarians (to be mentioned in a moment), southeastern colonials about the end of that century and all during the next sometimes had on their shelves the two best-known conservative political writers. Thomas Hobbes's *Leviathan* (1651) and other political discourses by him were in the Chesapeake provinces in the last decade of the seventeenth century and appear a number of times in the Carolinas in the eighteenth. Richard Lee II, owner of one of the large seventeenth-century libraries, which included Hobbes's *Philosophical Rudiments Concerning Government and Society* (1651) and his *De Corpore Politico; or The Elements of Law, Moral, and Politic* (1650), as a staunch royalist must have approved of the notions they advanced of government by the aristocracy and monarchy. How he differentiated between Hobbes and that other conservative author

Robert Filmer (in *Observations Concerning the Original of Government* [1652] and the now more famous *Patriarcha* [1680]), who disagreed with Hobbes on the means of acquiring absolute monarchical power in government and presented classic defenses of the status quo of Charles I, is not known. Filmer, who had a brother resident in Virginia, was represented on eighteenth-century southern shelves, as on those of Robert "King" Carter, Richard Bland, George Gilmer, and Thomas Jefferson. Libertarian Dr. Gilmer's commonplace book shows how thoroughly the physician had read and how deeply he detested Filmer's theories. The loyalist Reverend Jonathan Boucher of Maryland in *A View of the Causes and Consequences of the American Revolution* (1797) wrote, however, what Peter Laslett has called "the best common-sense defense of Filmer that ever was made."

John Locke's *Two Treatises on Government* (1690) was on a southern bookshelf before 1701. Boucher rejected Locke's theories, but until very recently the latter has been hailed as "America's philosopher," the political thinker who led us to the Declaration of Independence and gave us some of its phrases. Locke's libertarian and logical ideas, including his contract-compact theory of government (too familiar to be discussed here), were in southern libraries well before the end of the seventeenth century. In the past generation several historians reassessing our political heritage have shown rather conclusively that the works of Trenchard and Gordon were of greater influence, however, and were more widely known. One distinguished scholar states flatly that he can see no discernible evidence of the influence of Locke's governmental ideas in America before the mid-eighteenth century, and to support his contention cites the scarcity of copies of *Two Treatises* in the colonies before that date. This scholar may not have considered the fact that the collected editions of Locke's *Works* (1714, 1722, 1727, and 1740) contain the two political works and that, from at latest the 1730s, these editions were in Maryland,

Virginia, and both Carolinas. Also, they were referred to or quoted in southern newspapers over a long period. It is highly likely that Locke's insistence on moral law in politics, that no government could take its subjects' property without consent, and the other now familiar principles he expressed were at least well known in the colonial South well before 1750.

Algernon Sidney's *Discourses Concerning Government* (1698), published after this radical Whig's "martyrdom" (execution) and directed toward "constitutional restrictions and readjustments" which would strip the monarchy of any arbitrary prerogative and redistribute political power in accordance with property, and expressing the belief that rebellion is often necessary (among other now familiar concepts), was in the eighteenth century frequent in southern libraries and continued so through at least the first national period. His book was owned by Robert "King" Carter in 1732 and by his grandson Robert of Nomini two generations later, by William Byrd II and Richard Bland and Thomas Jefferson, by North Carolina Governor Thomas Burke, South Carolinian Joseph Wragg, various library societies, and later by John Taylor of Caroline and Judge Spencer Roane and Benjamin Watkins Leigh, and dozens more north and south. His title-page motto was adopted by Massachusetts as its motto, but Sidney was no more popular in New England than in the Southeast.

The strong Tory principles behind Samuel Butler's famous verse satire *Hudibras* (1663–1678) were probably not entirely the reason for its enormous popularity in all the colonies below the Susquehannah. Its targets were human foibles as well as political principles, and it offered quotable lines for those of any party persuasion. Though only a few copies are recorded before 1700, the familiarity with its meter and phrases and persona shown by later seventeenth-century southern colonial writers is sufficient evidence of its presence. Actually there are more copies of *Hudibras* in libraries throughout the eighteenth century than of any other English poem in all five provinces. Obviously read more for its politics, yet curiously listed by some historians (who should know better) simply as travel literature, is Robert Viscount Molesworth's *An Account of Denmark as It Was in the Year 1692* (1694), a depiction by a deeply troubled libertarian of the nature and development of absolutism, the story of how a near neighbor of England gradually lost its representative government to a despotic monarchy. Caroline Robbins says that Molesworth was the most influential and widely quoted of the Real or Liberal Whigs during his lifetime and for a considerable period thereafter. In the South he is most evident in libraries inventoried about the middle of the eighteenth century, though he is still present in 1800. In the 1750s he was referred to in Virginia's satiric "Dinwiddianae" poems, protesting a royal governor's arbitrary exercise of prerogative. The poet appends a note recommending that every "true British Subject" read this book, especially for its examples of unjust taxation.

Frequently referred to were continental European political commentators Samuel von Puffendorf and Charles Louis de Secondat, baron de Montesquieu. Puffendorf, historian and lawyer and philosopher, as well as political writer, published editions of most of his work before his death in 1694, though many of his books were reprinted throughout the eighteenth century in Latin and English. The *De Jure Naturae et Gentium* and its resume', *De Officio Hominis et Civis Juxta Legem Naturalem,* as well as *An Introduction to the Principal States and Kingdoms of Europe,* were in many libraries, medium and large and social or public in all five colonies. Among other principles, Puffendorf held that public law was not to be regarded as the will of the state but as the sum of individual wills (thus anticipating Rousseau), and that the state of nature is not one of war (as Hobbes believed) but of peace. Equally ubiquitous and perhaps more influential were several works of Montesquieu, especially French and English editions of his *Persian Letters* (orig. ed. 1721) and *Spirit of the Laws* (orig. ed.

1748). His discussions of the feedback and interplay between society and government, between natural environment and civilization, represent the subtlety and elusiveness of some eighteenth-century political expressions. Presbyterian parson Samuel Davies read him with pleasure but obviously without much understanding. Dr. George Gilmer quotes with approval his well-known aphorism, "Where law ends, tyranny begins." Today, Howard Mumford Jones calls him an arch conservative, and another commentator, presumably agreeing with Jones, notes that he had a far-reaching effect on the framers of the Constitution. At Princeton, Madison studied *The Spirit of the Laws* as a textbook. Jefferson changed his mind about Montesquieu as the years passed, though as early as 1790 he warned his son-in-law that though *The Spirit of the Laws* was usually recommended for its presentation of the science of government, it was as full of political heresies as of truth. In his student's commonplace book, Jefferson had copied many passages from this political and legal philosopher, but by 1810 he gave an even lower opinion of the book than he had in 1790. In 1811 he was sufficiently pleased with a considerably revised edition by Destutt de Tracy to write a "proem" for its first (Philadelphia) publication, underlining the paradoxes and misconceptions or misstatements of the original and declaring "Tracy's Review of Montesquieu, the ablest work which the last century has given us." Though a recent writer on the American Enlightenment sees Montesquieu as the most often praised and cited major French figure, one gathers from a brief survey of southern comments that the baron was never as frequently quoted in this area as in other colonies. The subject is perhaps worth investigation.

Of the half-dozen most popular writers on politics and government in the eighteenth-century South only one, John Locke, has so far been discussed. All the remaining five published their comments within the century and were strikingly varied in the literary forms they used. One wrote a tragic drama with a Roman title and setting; another wrote a French novel with classical origins, bearing as title the name of an ancient hero; the third wrote essays under the pseudonym "Cato," and later his own political discourses, with his translation of the Roman historian Tacitus. The fourth writer's major work in prose is as well known for its aesthetic and social philosophy as for its political, and the fifth's is a pseudo-Whig journal as well as a study of the idea of a patriot king; the last writer is usually labeled either as a Tory or as a most conservative Whig.

Joseph Addison, major Whig statesman and, with Pope, the most popular secular writer in the colonies throughout the eighteenth century, produced in 1712 and published in 1713 the first great neoclassical tragedy under the title *Cato*. Written from a Whig perspective, it was capable of being adopted by Tories as well as Whigs as a presentation of the impeccable model of patriotism and virtue. As with other neoclassical literature, its purpose was didactic, "to inculcate virtue." The protagonist may be entirely too admirable in his inflexibility against tyranny and in his magnanimity toward his enemies, but he was the ideal of readers and theatergoers in Britain and America for a full century. On the stage *Cato* was enormously popular in the New World. It was a favorite in the southern colonies in private theatricals, as George Washington remembered on the battlefield during the French and Indian War—as he wrote to the lady who had once been the great love of his life. An inveterate playgoer, Washington had probably seen this drama many times on the professional stage. Some time before 1748 he scribbled verse in his notebook, paraphrasing lines from the play, and his letters during the Revolution contain at least one quotation from it. Long after his presidency he quoted eight lines, including two which were also favorites of his contemporary Landon Carter:

> *'When vice prevails, and impious men bear sway,'*
> The post of honour is a private station [IV, iv, 142–143].

Strolling players had presented *Cato* professionally in Charleston in 1735 and students of William and Mary pro-

duced it in the Williamsburg theater in 1736. It appeared again
and again in public performances along the Atlantic coast at
Annapolis, Charleston, Baltimore, New York, and Philadelphia, as late as the season 1837–1838. It was quoted in essays in
all the southern provincial gazettes, and many political writers
used the pseudonym "Cato," as did Trenchard and Gordon in
their famous *Letters* (soon to be noted). School children in the
"Rev. Mr. Warrington's School" in Elizabeth City parish in
Virginia presented the play in 1767 with an original prologue
rendered by the rector's daughter:

> If nothing please you else, you'll clap the zeal
> Of brats who pant to serve the common weal.

One must remember too that at St. John's Church in Richmond Patrick Henry in 1775 echoed five lines of *Cato* (at least
as his biographer William Wirt presents his speech) in the
famous peroration ending "give me liberty or give me death."
And it was not by accident that it was one of the two plays
presented at Valley Forge during the crucial winter of
1777/1778.

Separately and in the collected *Works* of Addison, *Cato* was
in southern libraries from Daniel McCarty's and Robert
"King" Carter's time (before 1724) to at least the mid-nine-
teenth century. It is advertised for sale, with and without the
remainder of Addison's writings, in the Maryland, Virginia,
Carolina, and Georgia gazettes. The *Works* were owned not
only by scores of individuals but also by the Georgia Library
Society, the Charleston Library Society, and the Baltimore
Library Company. Addison's plays were recommended for any
beginning library in 1771 by Thomas Jefferson. His father had
owned them long before.

Almost as popular in the southern colonies was the treatise
in novel form by François de Salignac de la Motte Fénelon,
archbishop of Cambrai. *Les Aventures de Télémaque* (1699),
and soon in English translation as *The Adventures of Telema-*

chus, this "continuation" of the travels of the son of Ulysses in search of a father has of course classical roots. Not meant to be a liberal paper, it is a utopian and fairly easygoing compromise between dreams and possibilities. Its object had originally been to broaden the mind of the heir to the French throne. One feature that attracted Anglo-American libertarians was its advertisement of the doctrine that kings exist for the people rather than the other way around, as Clinton Rossiter has phrased it. By 1759 it had gone through seventeen editions in English. Even some French editions were published in London. But though today it is difficult to see any trace of a belief in liberty of conscience, as ascribed to its author by eighteenth-century readers, perhaps through the familiar process of wishful thinking it was so interpreted. A Scottish-born Virginia tutor in 1769 quoted a long passage from it in French, concerning the eternal punishment of a tyrannical king who had mistreated his slaves, a passage to support this southern colonial's own strictures on African slavery and miscegenation.

Not later than the 1720s, *Télémaque,* in English or French, was in all the southern colonies. It was owned by governors of North Carolina and Virginia, by schoolmasters, physicians, lawyers, clergymen (Anglican and dissenting), and planters. Byrd and Jefferson had copies in French, Washington in English. Politician James Milner of North Carolina and a dozen or more Carolina planters possessed French editions. The library companies held copies, and in 1797 the Lunenburg County, Virginia, country store still had it for sale. There are references to it and quotations from it in all the southern newspapers. Yet no one appears to have made a study in depth and breadth as to the reasons for its presence on the bookshelves.

Recent political historians have emphasized the influences of several works by Thomas Gordon and his older collaborator John Trenchard, usually allowing them an impression on eighteenth-century American ideology once assigned to John Locke. Certainly the two series of essays they did together, the *Independent Whig* and *Cato's Letters* (originally appearing in

serial form, the former going through seven collected editions
from 1721 to 1754 [not counting American issues of 1724 and
1740] and the latter through at least six in the same period),
were more frequently found on southern bookshelves than was
Locke on government, at least as far as our present knowledge
goes. They have been written about extensively by Caroline
Robbins, David L. Jacobson, and Bernard Bailyn (among
others). Thomas Gordon's translation of Tacitus (1728), which
included "Political Discourses," was almost as popular and
frequently quoted as the two collections of essays. In addition,
Gordon translated Sallust in 1744 and Trenchard published *A
Short History of Standing Armies* as early as 1698. Various
other works of the two men also appear occasionally in southern libraries.

These libertarian writers and their friends (such as Molesworth) were known as the Independent or Real or Radical
Whigs. Their two collections of essays are anticlerical or anti–
High Church, adamant against standing armies as instru-
ments of monarchical tyranny, anti-Catholic and anti-Stuart,
and concerned with the characters of good and evil magistrates
and the nature of human liberty and equality, declaring that
governments were instituted by men rather than "revealed" by
God, and warning of the dangers of liberty which might lead
to tyranny through factions and parties, among other things.
Their *Whig* and *Cato* spoke vehemently and effectively. The
two series owed much to Sidney's *Discourses* and earlier republican expressions. Americans found out immediately that these
essays could be adapted to their needs, and they were frequently
used in the Peter Zenger freedom-of-the-press controversy in
New York in the 1730s. Also in New York (somewhat later), the
Independent Reflector of William Livingston was patterned in
part on the *Whig.* "The Good Magistrate" in *Cato's Letters*
No. 37 (quoted from Sidney) appears in the *South Carolina
Gazette,* among other newspapers, in 1736, 1745, and 1749. The
Letters were quoted by North Carolinian Maurice Moore in a

1765 pamphlet against taxation of the colonies. George Mason seems to refer to the *Letters* in a 1766 essay and a 1774 resolution. Both *Cato's Letters* and the *Whig* appear on the shelves of private libraries in every southern colony and are advertised for sale in all their gazettes. They were also in the library societies from 1750 through at least 1798.

Though Thomas Jefferson's library, sold to Congress in 1814, contained these two collected essays of Trenchard and Gordon, the author of the Declaration appears to have been more interested in Gordon's translation of Tacitus, with its added political discourses and emphasis on the libertarian nature of German or Saxon government as the Roman historian wrote about it. The original discourses were indeed a distillation of Gordon's earlier work—for example, in its discussion of the relation of ministers, princes, and peoples; of free and arbitrary governments and the excellency of a limited monarchy; of the revolutionary nature of religion; of freedom of speech and the danger of standing armies. In Jefferson's opinion, Tacitus was "the first writer in the world without a single exception." He advised that because of the difficulty of the Latin it should be read with an English translation, and he declared that Gordon, of all translators, had best caught the spirit of the original. His own set of Tacitus was a conflated collection, combining a 1674 Latin printing with the second (1737) edition of Gordon.

In 1733 Stephen Bordley of Maryland wrote to England for a set of Gordon's first edition of Tacitus, and Daniel Dulany the elder, of the same colony, had this edition in his library. The 1796 library of Edward Lloyd IV also contained Gordon's translation. In Williamsburg in 1750–1752 Lewis Burwell bought this Tacitus at the *Gazette* bookshop, and as late as 1806 William Wirt ordered it from a sales catalogue of the Ralph Wormeley library. Georgians and Carolinians had Gordon's Tacitus, and dozens more in all the southern colonies had Latin versions.

Gradually all the volumes of Gordon and Trenchard disappeared from the southern (and American) bookshelf and were almost forgotten until recent historians searching for American ideological roots rediscovered them. Not only has the almost ubiquitous presence of these books been noted from inventories but we have become conscious of the frequent quotations from them of our eighteenth-century political leaders. The familiar principles of the American revolutionists were probably suggested by or derived from the writings of these men as much as from any other writers of the century.

Almost as well known, as frequently quoted, and as often on bookshelves was *Characteristics of Men, Manners, Opinions, Times, etc.* by Anthony Ashley Cooper, earl of Shaftesbury, a collection gathered and published by its author in 1711. Its best-known constituent, the previously separately published *Inquiry Concerning Virtue* (1709), is perhaps to be considered more philosophic, aesthetic, and religious than political, though as usual it is impossible to separate these elements. A Latitudinarian Christian who abhorred Hobbes and had been tutored by John Locke, whom he held in affection and respect, Shaftesbury rejected the mechanistic universe and Locke's tabula rasa. Admirably tolerant, he defended free-thinkers and was, on the same principle, anti-Puritanical. To find what the mind said, one had to see what the heart said; that is, man has a natural moral sense. The *Characteristics* as a whole, comments one critic, read like the work of an enraptured deist. Actually, he professed himself a theist. His philosophy, including its optimism, influenced Bolingbroke (next to be considered), the poet James Thomson, the French political theorist Montesquieu, and Americans such as Thomas Jefferson who were perhaps by nature as sanguine as Shaftesbury. His "homespun philosophy" of warning against "enthusiasm" (in our terms "fanaticism"), of declaring that all beauty is truth, of exaltation of nature, and of conviction of the necessity of freedom of thought made him a pioneer figure in all forms of romanticism, including the political. He was not democratical, he was monarchical; but he also advocated free institutions and a general liberalizing of public and private life. A confused and elegant writer, Howard Mumford Jones calls him, but he seems to have struck responsive chords in the minds of southern colonial Americans other than Jefferson, others who owned and quoted his great collection of essays. Like Fénelon and some of the British Real Whigs, he believed that mankind is capable of obtaining, or at least pursuing, happiness in this life.

The *Characteristics* was owned in every southern province and was frequently offered for sale by local booksellers. Clergymen (including orthodox Anglicans), sheriffs, merchants, and of course dozens of planters, among them William Byrd II, had copies in several volumes. Before 1740, William Dunlop, son of a University of Glasgow professor and owner of a large library that held this work, had a framed portrait (probably a print) of Shaftesbury on his wall, alongside portraits of Bolingbroke and Milton and Sir William Temple. Pre-Revolutionary activists who owned the book were the elder Gadsden, Richard Bland, and James Milner, in three different colonies.

Henry St. John Viscount Bolingbroke, who published *Remarks on the History of England* (1743) and *Letters on the Study and Use of History* (1752), is perhaps best remembered for his philosophical essays and especially for his studies in politics. Though he may not seem of first importance today in any of his chosen fields, the major minds—and many others—of his century held his talents in highest regard. Chesterfield and Pope were among them, and in America, Thomas Jefferson declared his style of the highest order, "the finest example in the English language of the eloquence proper for the senate." He added that Bolingbroke's political tracts were safe reading for the most timid religionist. These pronouncements from the great democrat may for some reasons seem astonishing, for Bolingbroke was a Jacobite aristocrat who rejected the liberal

ideology of Locke's *Second Treatise on Civil Government* and
Locke's bourgeois conception of natural right. Yet this British
"conservative Whig," as he has been called, held and widely
expressed many ideas with which Jefferson and, even more,
John Adams and many southern Revolutionists less liberal
than Jefferson or the English Real Whigs might agree. Bolingbroke's family-centered aristocracy had much in common in
theory and practice with the practice and ideas of many southern planters, as did his antagonism to the moneyed interests,
the court party, which he felt had replaced the natural rulers,
the rural gentry. With southern colonials, he early held the
Harringtonian economic-political view, though he replaced it
in his *Dissertation upon Parties* (1735) and *Letters on the
Spirit of Patriotism; or the Idea of a Patriot King* (1749, but
available earlier) with concepts that owed something to Machiavelli. This English nobleman was ready to find the principle
of party acceptable if that party represented the interests of the
whole nation (he felt that the Walpole Whigs represented only
one class). His remedy for England's problems was a patriot
king who would be the restorer of a mixed government, in all
of which Machiavelli and the cyclical theory of history were
involved.

Many of Bolingbroke's works originally appeared in a periodical, the *Craftsman* (14 vols. from 1726–1736). Opposed even
to the idea of standing armies, he joined—on their far right—
the neo-Harringtonians or Real Whigs, aligning himself
within limits with these libertarians who had Molesworth and
Trenchard and Gordon at their extreme left. His savage attacks
in the *Craftsman* on the Walpole administration were often
indistinguishable from the writings of Trenchard and Gordon,
and in fact he frequently quoted them. Bailyn has pointed out
how close his concept of the English constitution or the idea of
a constitution was to John Adams's, and there were certainly
southern delegates to the Constitutional Convention of 1787
who held similar views.

Jefferson, who may not have agreed fully with Bolingbroke on constitutions and certainly not on aristocracy, owned a remarkable number (13) of the Englishman's writings. He had first editions of *Reflections Concerning Innate Moral Principles* (1752) and *The Philosophical Works* (5 vols., 1754); early editions of two volumes of the *Craftsman* (1727); *A Letter to Sir William Windham* (1753), which includes a letter to Pope and "Some Reflections on the Present State of the Nation"; *A Collection of Political Tracts* (1748), including papers from the *Craftsman*; *A Dissertation upon Parties* (1754), reprinted separately from 1733–1734 issues of the journal; some editions of the *Patriot King* (now lost); *The Craftsman Extraordinary* (1729); *The Second Craftsman Extraordinary* (1729); *Remarks on the History of England* (1745), also from the *Craftsman;* *Letters on the Study and Use of History* (1752); and another work possibly by St. John. Undoubtedly, Bolingbroke's influence was strongest on this American's moral and religious beliefs. William Byrd II had all fourteen volumes of the *Craftsman,* as did two members of the Custis family. Landon Carter owned at least two of Bolingbroke's books, and John Mercer had some of his works at Marlborough. Even Mrs. Charles Stagg, widow of the first producer of plays at Williamsburg, owned seven volumes of the *Craftsman.* In Maryland, Bolingbroke appears in the collections of Stephen Bordley, Charles Carroll of Carrollton, Edward Lloyd IV, and others of lesser note. He also appears several times in North Carolina and often on South Carolina bookshelves, with at least five titles in the Charleston Library Society. Bolingbroke's combination of an elegant and refreshing style, his appeal to the agrarian or country element of society, and his opposition on many grounds to the British political establishment, which from the 1730s many colonials felt was oppressing them, is the most obvious explanation of his appeal to many southern Americans. Presbyterian clergyman Samuel Davies mentions him in one sermon, but merely to call him an infidel. I have not chanced upon any title by Bolingbroke in any clerical library, Anglican or dissenting.

In lesser quantities but fairly widespread throughout the southern colonies were a number of other Anglo-European treatises on politics, from most of which the southern eighteenth-century colonial, growing more and more restless from what he considered home-government encroachment, drew some nourishment. They include Whig Bishop Benjamin Hoadly's sermons and tracts; the Italian Cesar Beccaria's *Crimes and Punishments* (1st English trans. 1767; it was one of three books by Italian authors reprinted in English in the eighteenth century, one instance being Charleston in 1777), "a small gem of the Enlightenment" which Jefferson read before the Revolution; Jonas Hanway's *An Historical Account of the British Trade Over the Caspian Sea,* actually a study in crime and politics referred to in a Virginia verse satire of the 1750s; Lord George Lyttelton's several historical political pieces; Giovanni Marana's *Letters of the Turkish Spy;* Bernard Mandeville's *Fable of the Bees;* John Milton's prose tracts; James Thomson's Whig poem *Liberty;* and perhaps above all, Henry Care's *English Liberties,* referred to by Nicholas Trott, George Mason, Daniel Dulany, Jr., and Thomas Jefferson.

Not only are southern political theories explicitly or implicitly stated in their legislative records from 1607 to 1800, but the seventeenth-century promotion and historical accounts from the colonies include direct references to government. By 1701 an anonymous Virginian had published in London *An Essay upon the Government of the English Plantations on the Continent of America,* a perceptive analysis of problems facing the colonies and suggestions for remedies. Recent scholars assign it on external or internal evidence to Virginia planter Ralph Wormeley or Benjamin Harrison III. It shows Whig leanings and perhaps some influence of Locke's *Two Treatises.* It is found on several southern bookshelves, as are the first Daniel Dulany's *Right of the Inhabitants of Maryland to the Benefit of the English Laws* (1728) and the later pre-Revolutionary, Revolutionary, and Constitutional essays on political science of the second Daniel Dulany, Charles Carroll of Carrollton, Landon Carter and Richard Bland and John Camm and Jonathan Boucher, Maurice Moore and William Borden and Henry McCulloh, Henry Laurens and Christopher Gadsden and William Henry Drayton, and John J. Zubly. During the last quarter of the eighteenth century, beginning with Jefferson's *Summary View of the Rights of British America,* through Arthur Lee and St. George Tucker and James Madison's great *Federalist* essays, and into the Federalist-Republican debates of the 1790s, southerners wrote on politics and read their own and other's comments. Tucker's Americanized edition of Blackstone represents all three of the major areas of expression represented in this chapter; Ramsay's speeches and histories are also politics, as is the South Carolina–Georgia history of Alexander Hewatt.

Not all eighteenth-century colonists in our region possessed legal tomes, but a large number did. Almost all who owned ten books or more were likely to have one or more histories on their shelves, and the larger libraries had scores if not hundreds, most of them capable of being interpreted as libertarian in viewpoint. Clearly the political pamphlets and books were predominantly Whiggish, of the fairly extreme radical variety. As early as 1740 Virginian William Dunlop possessed a library which may only be designated as libertarian, for he possessed the histories and philosophies and political commentaries of almost every radical Whiggish writer here mentioned. William Byrd II, whose son was to be a loyalist, possessed more libertarian than conservative or monarchical volumes, though in his large library he had studies in many politcal hues. John Mercer's collection is definitely Whiggish, as one might expect from the probable author of the satiric "Dinwiddianae" poems. Libertarian in most of their titles are smaller private libraries and such social libraries as those in Charleston and Baltimore. One cannot say that the books on their shelves shaped the majority of eighteenth-century southern political concepts in 1701, in the quarter century just before the Revolution, in the decade before the adoption of the federal Constitution, or in the party-divided final decade of the century. But these southern Americans had in the books of their personal or club libraries and in copious extracts in their newspapers materials which could influence their thinking or bolster the opinions preconceived from experience. Not all of their reading matter was liberal or republican or anti-imperial, but neither were all of them. Despite the loyalist stance and arguments of a Jonathan Boucher in Maryland and several gentlemen of prominence in all the other southern colony-states, however, the fact is that the people of this area in general found the libertarian writers most congenial to their agrarian way of life and the peculiar colonial problems of taxation and government. They saw the Saxon or German agrarian past as a republican golden age which suggested a secular as well as the familiar cyclical interpretation of man's history, an interpretation which included a secular millennial progress. Perhaps Puritan New Englanders and Quaker Philadelphians and New York Calvinists could develop their libertarian ideas from a more religious or theological form of historical cycle, or in reaction from their earlier acceptance of the Christian explanation, but despite the existence of slavery in the region, the southerner felt that his secular legal-historical-political reading indicated an obvious continuity of the basic concept of individual right in his New World society.

TWO

Religion

IN OUR CENTURY A NUMBER OF THOUGHTFUL COMMENTATORS, including Allen Tate, have declared that "convinced supernaturalism" has been and is a dominant characteristic of the southern mind. In part this belief comes from present-day observation, in part perhaps from a delayed reaction to certain nineteenth-century claims that early New England had left or had imposed upon us in all America, an essentially religious cast of thought. The nineteenth-century historians, and some in our own age, have contrasted a vigorous and sustained New England Puritan cerebration in theological doctrine and morality with an allegedly equally sustained lackadaisical or indifferent southern attitude toward matters spiritual. Recent critical scholarship, such as that of Allen Tate or Donald Davidson, has done much to qualify or correct the generalization about the historical South. But only occasionally and briefly has the problem, for such it is, been approached through a look at the reading habits and reading matter of southerners during the first two centuries of their region's existence, the same period in which whatever patterns came from New England were formed. Several good general studies of early southern reading such as those mentioned in the introduction above are useful, but only a few scholars, notably Louis B. Wright, have focused on religious material, and in his case primarily on seventeenth-century reading matter in one colony. More significant may be a look here at southern religious reading in the five colonies of the eighteenth century, when they were determining their own character as well as supplying major leaders in the formation of the Republic.

But long before this the first Jamestown colonists were establishing their precarious existence, armed with Bibles, Testaments, Books of Common Prayer and printed sermons, along with muskets and swords and pikes. In the first two years, 1607–1608, an early president of the resident council was accused of atheism because he appeared to have no Bible, and he himself described, for authorities back in London, his frantic search in his trunk or chest for his copy of God's word, which he claimed had been maliciously stolen. In two letters back home in the 1620s, Richard Freethorne, an artisan, quotes directly from the Bible he has before him. And in the whole period under the Virginia Company of London before 1624 the records show a steady flow of imported Bibles, Books of Common Prayer, works of piety such as Lewis Bayly's popular old-fashioned theological *The Practise of Pietie* (c. 1613), collected editions of sermons by well-known theologians such as Gervase Babington and Henry Smith and William Perkins, Ursinus's *Catechism* (1591), and even Saint Augustine's *City of God* in Latin or English. That the several clergymen who accompanied the first settlers had fairly extensive and comprehensive theological libraries is indicated by a direction from authorities in Britain that an impoverished young minister, just going to the New World, be supplied with books from those of the clergy who had recently died, books which were said to be abundantly present.

During the remainder of the seventeenth century, as Maryland and the Carolinas came into existence and population increased in the first four southern colonies, works such as these continued to be imported. New collections of sermons, books of devotion, and doctrinal discussions appear in the inventories. They are also mentioned in such letters as those of William Fitzhugh, ordering books from London. Naturally, most of those new and some of the older books usually bore

English imprints, but there are some Scottish and a few Irish imprints, and in Maryland and South Carolina especially, books that were published in France and the Netherlands. Undoubtedly, there were in seventeenth-century Maryland several good collections of theological treatises written for and by Roman Catholics. The Jesuit missionaries and the Catholic group around the proprietor's governor were far outnumbered from the beginning, however, by Protestants, and there is legal record of a Roman Catholic planter of the ruling group who was disciplined or fined for forbidding his indentured servant's reading of a Protestant theological work. By the time the Carolinas were chartered and organized, the Commonwealth interregnum and a related successful rebellion by Puritan elements in Maryland had ensured the proclaimed tolerance of all Christian sects in that province. The known inventories of the century are usually Protestant in tone, and Wheeler gives no predominantly Roman Catholic theological collection in his studies of later Maryland reading and libraries.

German and French Huguenot groups, beginning to settle in the Southeast before the end of the first century, certainly brought religious books in their own languages as well as in Latin or Hebrew or Greek and continued to do so throughout the eighteenth century. But in an overwhelming majority of libraries throughout the South from the beginning to 1800, the omnipresent book was the Bible and/or the New Testament, most frequently accompanied by, even in dissenting households, the Anglican Book of Common Prayer and Anglican or Presbyterian or Lutheran catechisms and varied books of devotion. Many of the larger libraries, running into scores or hundreds of titles, including those of planters and physicians and lawyers and merchants, contained a high percentage of religious works; those under twenty volumes were almost always predominantly religious, and those of three or four books usually entirely so. This would not be remarkable even for New or Old England, for it is estimated that almost half the titles published in Great Britain through 1640 were theological.

As the seventeenth century wore on, new editions of older works were added to southeastern libraries. John Calvin's *Institutes of the Christian Religion* and other writings of the great Genevan were in several Virginia libraries before the middle of the century, in both clerical and lay collections, and they continued to have a place on Anglican as well as Presbyterian shelves through the eighteenth century (John Mercer the lawyer and Thomas Jefferson owned Calvin's treatises). The church fathers, including Saint Augustine and Thomas Aquinas and a dozen others, were reprinted in both the seventeenth and the eighteenth centuries and found their way into clerical and lay libraries. Presbyterians and Anglicans and Catholics owned several of them in the first century. A hundred and more years later, James Madison, who had read widely the church fathers under Witherspoon at Princeton and had many titles in his personal library, sent Jefferson a formidable list of their works to be bought for the new University of Virginia library, almost all in seventeenth-century editions. Southern colonials also bought the works of Puritan authors, such as the treatises of William Ames and the sermons of noted Puritan preachers.

Appearing in every colony and taking its place on the shelf beside the Bible and Book of Common Prayer was the Cambridge *Concordance to the Bible* (with varying title and editors, first printed 1631), whose most popular edition was edited by a nonconformist who emigrated to New England. It was still reprinted and sold in the eighteenth century (Thomas Jefferson owned two versions). But next to the Bible, and frequently in dissenting as well as Anglican libraries, was Richard Allestree's *The Whole Duty of Man, Laid down in a plain and Familiar Way for the Use of All, but especially the Meanest Reader,* published anonymously in 1658. This handbook of Christian ethics and devotions went through edition after edition, through and beyond the American Revolution. It was reprinted by William Parks at Williamsburg in 1746, and all the colonial gazettes frequently advertised it for sale. It was in libraries sent by Dr. Bray to the colonies at the end of the seventeenth century. For example, it was in the parochial collections at Huguenot Manicantown in Virginia in 1710 and at Pamplico in North Carolina in 1700. It was also in the library sent to catechist Joseph Ottolenghe in Georgia in 1753 by Dr. Bray's Associates. Usually it was sent in multiple copies: 187 copies to the Georgia colony from an unknown benefactress in 1733 and thirteen to Augusta's first library in 1750, and long before, in 1701, at least three hundred to Bray's own colony of Maryland. Bray intended that it be included in all S.P.G. libraries in America. Landon Carter in 1778 had the twenty-first edition, and later Jefferson's library catalogue indicates its presence.

Next to Allestree's book in numbers among devotional volumes were two by Richard Baxter, who, though "tainted" by nonconformity, was well represented in Anglican as well as Presbyterian and even Quaker libraries by *The Saints Everlasting Rest* (1650) and *A Call to the Unconverted* (1657). John Carter II of Virginia, presumably an orthodox Anglican, had six of Baxter's works, as well as a book by a John Ball, who was, like Baxter, a tolerant or middle-of-the-road Puritan. Carter also had William Penn's *No Cross, No Crown* (1669), a famous Quaker work which often stood on the shelf beside the Book of Common Prayer and the Cambridge *Concordance*. The number of unorthodox religious books increased in Anglican libraries in the eighteenth century. In the late seventeenth, their presence may suggest an early southern religious tolerance, but more probably a curiosity about nonconformity and the ethical and scriptural materials on which its various doctrines were based.

The number of pro- and anti-Quaker titles in all sorts of public and private southern libraries suggests several things, among them the historical fact that the Friends were a most

active and numerous element in the southern colonies from the
late 1670s to the Revolution. Their great missionaries, George
Fox, William Edmundson, John Woolman, John Burnyeat,
and especially Thomas Story, worked in the southeastern
colonies and wrote about them in volumes that soon were
scattered throughout the region. But Robert Barclay, once
called by Coleridge the Saint Paul of Quakerism, was better
represented than these missionaries by his *Apology for the
True Christian Divinity* (1678), the most famous of his several learned and orderly arguments. In 1724 a rural Virginia
Anglican clergyman, reporting to the bishop of London on the
spiritual state of his parish, pointed out his need of more
printed doctrinal materials for an enlarged parish library
because "shrew'd objectors among the quakers and even Deists
. . . [and] Robert Barclay's learning both filled [the mouths of
several persons] with some of the learned arguments against
the Bible." Without certain equally learned replies many "will
be caus'd to stumble," he warned. This Reverend Mr. Alexander Forbes had certainly read Barclay and probably, like Anglican Huguenot Parson Latané and Presbyterian Nathaniel
Taylor, owned a copy of the *Apology*. So did several planters,
as did two Custises and a Carter and a Wormeley and Thomas
Jefferson, and so did the Charleston Library Society. The
South Carolina library owned at least three other pro-Quaker
publications, which is not surprising if one remembers how
strong the Quakers had been in both Carolinas earlier in the
eighteenth century.

But far better known at the end of the seventeenth century
and down to the American Revolution were two polemical
works concerned with the Quakers by Charles Leslie, a cutting
satiric polemicist who also is remembered for a work against
the deists (to be noted below). In 1696 Leslie published the first
edition of *The Snake in the Grass; or Satan Transform'd into
an Angel of Light, Discovering the Deep and Unsuspected
Subtility which is couched under the Pretended Simplicity of*

Many of the Principal Leaders of those People call'd Quakers.
This was answered by Joseph Wyeth in *Anguis flagellatus; or,
A Switch for the Snake* . . . in 1699, and was replied to in turn
by Leslie in *The Defense of the Snake* in 1700 (with a revised
edition in 1702). Dr. Samuel Johnson commended Leslie as a
powerful reasoner, as apparently he was. Quaker Thomas
Story in his *Journal* (1747) rather humorously gives the inci-
dents of his own encounters with *The Snake* in Virginia and
Maryland, for he debated doctrine with Church of England
clergymen who brought the book against him, one parson in
Maryland in 1699 drawing the little book from his bosom as
though it were a lethal weapon. *The Snake* is found in Bray's
1698 parochial library, in 1700 in North Carolina's Brett Parish Library, in 1700 in the South Carolina Provincial Library,
and in the private libraries of a Presbyterian parson in 1709
and of William Byrd II in 1744.

Other seventeenth-century theological or religious works
continued to appear in libraries well into the next century:
William Cave's *A Dissertation Concerning the Government of
the Ancient Church* (1683), in the libraries of Presbyterian and
Anglican clergy, of Governor Francis Nicholson, of provincial
libraries in Annapolis and Charleston, and of private laymen;
Fox's *Book of Martyrs;* dozens or scores of sermon collections,
such as those of William Perkins, Jeremy Taylor, Edward
Stillingfleet, James Ussher, John Jewel, and John Wilkins; and
the major works on witchcraft by Perkins, Joseph Glanville,
and John Webster. The sermons represented many homiletic
forms and shades of opinion, political and doctrinal. William
Fitzhugh in the 1680s and the Rev. Dr. Francis Le Jau and
Chief Justice Trott early in the eighteenth century affirmed
their belief in witchcraft, and one or more of the learned
volumes on the subject were owned by Ralph Wormeley, John
Waller, Thomas Thompson, and William Byrd II among the
planters, by Trott, by Presbyterian parson Nathaniel Taylor,
and by North Carolina Governor Arthur Dobbs as late as 1765.

Southerner's knowledge of and relation to John Bunyan's *Pilgrim's Progress* (1678–1679) was brought up a century ago by historian Henry Adams in his *John Randolph* (1882). Adams says rather sneeringly that certainly John Randolph— for him the quintessential southerner—could not have liked and probably had never read Bunyan's book, which was a necessary commodity in every eighteenth-century *New England* farmhouse. Long ago William Cabell Bruce, in another biography of Randolph, cited letter after letter to prove that Randolph in his youth had read Bunyan and many years later strongly recommended it to a niece. Actually, *Pilgrim's Progress* appears in the library inventories of every southern colony and was advertised in the gazettes of these provinces late in the eighteenth century. It was one of two books the Baptist Reverend Isaac Chanler insisted in his will (1749) that his children have, and another Baptist's library of the same colony a year or two later certainly included Bunyan. Anglicans such as Mason L. Weems and William Duke also owned the book, and Anglican Catesby Cocke refers to the "Proem" in a letter of October 25, 1726. Catalogues of books for sale in Williamsburg, Charleston, Annapolis, and Savannah list it near the end of century. In the Alamance section of piedmont North Carolina in the 1790s, Scotch-Irish Presbyterian personal libraries included *Pilgrim's Progress,* as well as the works of Baxter and Watts and Fox's *Book of Martyrs.*

Though the titles and authors just mentioned indicate considerable continuity in theological reading, the end of the seventeenth century was marked by a new determined effort of the Anglican Society for the Propagation of the Gospel in Foreign Parts and the Society for the Propagation of Christian Knowledge to promote knowledge of religion by the establishment of libraries in British colonies throughout the world but especially in North America. Its impelling force was Dr. Thomas Bray, for a brief period (around 1700) resident commissary for the bishop of London in Maryland, a man who devoted his entire life to what has been called his grand design. To the S.P.C.K. and the S.P.G.—designed in the first instance to raise money for libraries and find ministers to be sent to the colonies, and in the second to distribute books and missionaries in the colonies in which the Church of England was not established—a third organization was added in 1728, Dr. Bray's Associates. The third group, among other activities, planned the founding of Negro schools in the colonies. In Virginia, because the church was there established, the first two organizations did little except supply a parish library for the Huguenots of Manicantown, but Dr. Bray's Associates were for a time quite successful in their schools for blacks established in such towns as Fredericksburg and Williamsburg.

The story of the establishment of laymen's and parish and provincial libraries has been told many times, though not yet quite fully. Though libraries were established as far north as Massachusetts and Rhode Island, the most successful and concentrated campaign was in Dr. Bray's Maryland. Between 1696 and 1704 Bray set up book collections in thirty-two parishes of that colony, the collection at St. Mary's being large enough to be called a provincial library, as was a later collection in Annapolis. In 1704 similar collections were given to Kikotan (Hampton) in Virginia and Albemarle in North Carolina. During the rest of the eighteenth century, through 1768, the S.P.G. set up parochial libraries from Maine south and west—with six in North Carolina, sixteen in South Carolina, and probably one more in Virginia. One of the collections in each of the Carolinas was large enough to be known as a provincial library. Dr. Bray's Associates also established a number of parochial collections between 1735 and 1771, most of them in connection with Negro schools. The various libraries were planned to supply sufficient theological material for the use of clergymen in preparing sermons or for debating militant nonconformists such as the Quakers, to aid laymen in attempting to comprehend Christian doctrine, to supply practical books to instruct laymen in their everyday occupations, and in the large provincial libraries to provide a wide range of research material for the active theologian and, in some instances, the intellectual layman.

All these collections contained the standard volumes already discussed, including several copies of *The Whole Duty of Man*, the Book of Common Prayer, and certain sermons. There were dozens of scriptural commentaries and doctrinal tracts and religious dictionaries and encyclopedias. *The Snake in the Grass*, Baker's *Chronicle of the Kings of England*, various volumes on heraldry or the peerage, George Keith's anti-Quaker pamphlets, the English satire *Hudibras*, Juvenal's *Satires* in Latin, several English histories, Boyle's medical experiments, and the *Art of Speaking* were in the large library that was sent to Bath in North Carolina in 1700, theoretically for Mr. Daniel Brett's parish alone but almost surely intended for a larger constituency which might be partly secular. The smaller collection that was sent to Manicantown in Virginia in 1710, on the other hand, was clearly intended for the use of the clergyman and pious laymen of the parish, for it was entirely theological, including, besides standard sermons and concordances and *The Whole Duty of Man*, such a practical volume as "Herbert's Country Parson" (London, 1652).

Most of the thousands of primarily religious volumes thus sent to the southern colonies have long since disappeared. Many were carelessly or indifferently handled, but there is good evidence that just as many were worn out with use. By 1724, in their reports to the bishop of London, most parish clergy complained that they needed replacements and additions, and some stated that they had never received the books to which they were entitled. But, especially in Maryland and the Carolinas, the books seem to have been in the hands of a remarkable number and variety of people. There were a few knotty morsels such as Calvin to chew on, but there were many straightforward, homely, practical devotionals and hundreds of edifying sermons for the Sundays on which the parson could not be present. They are aimed at a clergy and laity who did not believe in, and were not subject to, a theocratic state. They represent a form of Christian doctrinal piety which almost the dullest literate might comprehend and embrace. One suspects that volumes such as *The Whole Duty of Man* have left their quiet teachings in the oral or folk religion of the later South, and perhaps most obviously in the adaptations of Anglican liturgy and doctrine by their Methodist descendants.

One scholar writing on religion in eighteenth-century England calls it an age of repose in which men had time to debate religious questions but few reasons to fight over them. For America, whether men debated or fought becomes somewhat a matter of definition and geography. Alan Heimert has depicted New England in this period, especially from the 1730s, as a battleground, or at least a forensic, controversial-tract set-to between "liberal" Calvinists and "conservative" deists or Unitarians or Arminians. Beginning in Georgia, the great English Calvinist, Anglican evangelist George Whitefield, attempted for several decades to engage all the Atlantic coastal colonies in an evangelical crusade. In the South, he was somewhat successful in South Carolina and to a lesser extent in Maryland and Georgia, but in North Carolina and Virginia he did not find enough people sufficiently interested in forwarding or in combating his program to declare themselves in a body of polemical prose.

Books were very definitely, however, a part of the religious atmosphere of all the South before 1800. Of the 1,200 volumes in his orphan school at Bethesda in Georgia, Whitefield had 900 on religion. Though naturally they did not include any of the orthodox Anglican or other books that he had proscribed, they reflected religious reading tastes among many sorts of British Christians and were in many instances representative of traditional doctrine, though there was an emphasis on the Calvinist and Presbyterian and evangelical. As the Presbyterians and other militant Calvinists became stronger in the South, they stressed Richard Baxter and their own contemporaries Philip Doddridge and Isaac Watts, for prose tracts and hymns; some British poets, such as George Herbert and Edward Young (they shared them with the Anglicans); and even fellow Americans such as Jonathan Edwards. They also recommended certain Calvinist divines, though the New Light evangelicals differed from the Old Light conservatives considerably in their lists of homiletic reading.

Whitefield recommended certain books and condemned others, but except in the cases of two or three Charleston Baptist and Independent-Presbyterian clergy, there is little evidence that individuals attempted to follow his advice in stocking their shelves. Anglicans and Presbyterians (Quaker libraries have almost disappeared from the records) included old and new editions of the theologians already mentioned, as well as the works of some hitherto unmentioned Latitudinarian or deistic or rationalistic clergy of the end of the seventeenth century, their Trinitarian and pietist opponents in that period, and the followers of both in the eighteenth century. Actually, developing theology closely paralleled current concepts in politics, literature, and science in both the colonies and the mother country. Some intellectual historians see a parallel between neoclassicism and deism, for example, and certainly the Newtonian science was in some senses reflected in the rational theology, including Latitudinarian Arminianism, from the later seventeenth through the eighteenth century. The rational theologians were often the radical Whig theologians, such as Bishop Benjamin Hoadly, who wrote on civil government and *The Reasonableness of Conformity to the Church of England* (1703) and whose books were owned in the South by Presbyterian and Anglican clergy and by laymen from Maryland to Georgia. His book on conformity was in answer to another popular item on southern shelves, Edward Calamy's *Defense of Modern Nonconformity* (also 1703).

Varying shades of Arianism, Arminianism, Socinianism, deism, and even Trinitarianism are represented in the rational theology in the libraries of almost all the clergy, both dissenting and Anglican, in the southern colonies. Some of these doctrinal philosophies were employed as points of departure from or basic disagreement with the church establishment. Evangelicals Samuel Davies of Virginia and Josiah Smith of South Carolina so employed them. In laymen's libraries, too, rational theology appeared side by side with the literature of revelation. The long list of titles reflecting some degree of theological rationalism perhaps begins with John Wilkins's *Principles of Natural Religion* (1678), a moderate work anticipating many of the ideas popularized in Joseph Butler's *Analogy of Religion, Natural and Revealed, to the Constitution and Course of Nature* (1736), and proceeds through John Ray's *Wisdom of God in the Creation* (1691), Edward Stillingfleet's *Natural and Revealed Religion* (1719), William Wollaston's *Religion of Nature Delineated* (1722), and Shaftesbury's mild and ethical deism in *Charactaristics* and elsewhere to Joseph Priestley and Lord Kames (both were friends of Thomas Jefferson). Most frequently found in the Southeast were the books by Wollaston and Butler and Samuel Clarke.

The Arian Samuel Clarke was read widely north and south in the colonies, especially his *Demonstration of the Being and Attributes of God* (1705–1706), which includes in the rest of its long title "the truth and certainty of the Christian Revelation in Answer to Mr. Hobbes, Spinoza . . ." In other words, Christian doctrine and miracles, as the emanations from a divine being, conform to the teachings of sound and unprejudiced reason. His works were owned in every southern colony. Presbyterian Samual Davies, orthodox Calvinist, approvingly refers in his writings to "the celebrated Dr. Clarke" or "the great man." John Mackenzie in South Carolina, whose fine 1772 library catalogue survives, suggested to the younger William Henry Drayton, who liked to quote Pope on religion, that more might be learned of the deity from Dr. Clarke's sermon than from "the crampt sense of all the poets in this world." Maryland intellectual parson Thomas Cradock, poet and eloquent and orthodox Anglican preacher, owned at least two works of Clarke's in copies which yet survive. Thomas Jefferson had several of Clarke's books. Clarke's theological doctrines gave offense to extreme deists and anti-deists, but he was respected by most of his contemporaries in Britain and was in America, with Doddridge (especially in the North) and Tillotson, one of the three most widely read English divines, perhaps because to rational Augustan colonials he represented a compromise.

William Wollaston's "little textbook of ethics," which taught that the criterion of virtue is "conformity to the truth of things as they are," which was ridiculed by Franklin in his youth and by Jefferson in his old age, was in all five colonies. William Byrd II refers to the work in his commonplace book, and it was owned by John Mercer, Richard Bland, North Carolina Governor Martin, and Baltimore and Charleston library societies. Even more popular and enduring was Butler's *Analogy*, called by some the greatest apologetic work of the century and the greatest product of British ethical thought. It disarmed much criticism by its modesty and became a major weapon against "scientific deism." It was designed not so much to vindicate Christianity as to get deists not to reject it. Though Leslie Stephen observed that the *Analogy* made more sceptics than it redeemed, it was popular in the South with a great many people before and after the American Revolution, notably with Presbyterian Samuel Davies and early nationalist U.S. Attorney General William Wirt. Perhaps significantly, Butler leans to Calvinism of the variety with which these men and certain other southerners would have been in sympathy. The Library Company of Baltimore was still offering the book to its somewhat heterogeneous membership in 1798.

Two other rational theologians were read in the eighteenth-

century South. Matthew Tindal, a Christian deist of the order
of Sir John Randolph, published his *Christianity as Old as
Creation* in 1730. William Whiston, a scientist, and often
labeled an anti-Trinitarian, published the first of his volumi-
nous works, *A New Theory of the Earth,* in 1696. Far more
popular, at least in South Carolina, was the orthodox, plain
and practical *Expository Notes, with Practical Observations
on the New Testament* (1724) by William Burkitt, who person-
ally persuaded at least one missionary to go to South Carolina.
Of the thirty-five known copies in that colony, only one was
owned by a clergyman. "Burchet on the New Testament," as it
was designated in a shipment to Governor Francis Nicholson,
then in Charleston, went through nine editions in the eighteenth century and several more in the nineteenth. Burkitt
probably stood beside *The Whole Duty of Man* on southern
shelves.

Though George Whitefield declared Tillotson was not a
Christian and forbade his followers to read him, this good man
was far and away the most popular writer of sermons in the
colonial South, as he almost surely was in England. Archbishop of Canterbury and at least mildly Latitudinarian, he
composed discourses which were apparently an effective anti-
dote for unbelief. He declared that he wrote to show the
unreasonableness of atheism, the usefulness of religion to man,
the excellency of the Christian religion, and the need for man
to practice this "Holy religion." A collected *Works,* including
54 sermons and "The Rule of Faith" (orig. ed. 1691), was in its
ninth edition by 1728, and another collection of 254 sermons
was to be augmented and republished continuously through
the century. The first and longest homily, originally published separately and much earlier than 1691, is "The Wisdom
of Being Religious." Others are "The Advantage of Religion
to Societies," "The Hazard of Being Saved in the Church of
Rome," "The Distinguishing Character of Good and Bad
Men," "A Persuasion to Frequent Communion," and "Against

Evil-Speaking," all written in a persuasive, quiet, plain style. Tillotson appears many times in every colony and is in Governor Francis Nicholson's library in the Chesapeake Bay country by 1695, in the Bray libraries at least by 1698, in the Charleston Provincial Library in 1700–1712 (*The Posthumous Sermons*), in Burrington's Georgia collection before 1767, and in Jefferson's great library. Clergy, public officials, professional men, planters, library societies—all owned the *Works*. In 1740 Charleston merchant Robert Pringle ordered a complete set direct from London, though the South Carolina and other gazettes frequently advertise Tillotson for sale. Naturally commissary Alexander Garden of Charleston quoted and used Tillotson against Whitefield. Maryland Presbyterian parson Nathaniel Taylor had a "complete set" before 1709. Virginia satirist-legalist John Mercer of Marlborough owned the three volumes (presumably folio) of one edition by 1746.

Perhaps the best first hand evidence of the reading of Tillotson occurs in the writings of William Byrd II, who died in 1744. He read Tillotson on Sundays when there was no church service and sometimes during the week, perhaps alternating with the other books of "divinity" he mentions, usually without author or title. In April 1709: "We prepared to go to church, but the parson did not come, notwithstanding good weather, so I read in Dr. Tillotson at home." On a July Sunday he again "read a sermon of Dr. Tillotsons." And after periods of reading the millenarian prophecies of the bishop of Worcester and sermons by John Norris and (Henry?) Day, the following year he read many more Tillotson homilies. On one occasion he read a sermon and then had his wife read another aloud to him. Interspersed with "some divinity" (unidentified), Grotius, Bishop Latimer, and the New Testament, he continued to note Tillotson in his reading matter in 1711–1712 and in 1720 in his fragmentary *Diaries*. He also noted reading *The Whole Duty of Man*. A little more on Byrd and religion in a moment, but his testimony about Tillotson seems to suggest that this sophisticated southern planter and his fellows found in the great preacher the solace or guidance or edification they needed. There is indirect evidence too that Tillotson's homilies were favorites at Sunday services for reading aloud by laymen, in the frequent absence of ordained clergy, in the extensive southern parishes of the century.

Though the great dissenters Isaac Watts and Philip Dodd-ridge and the Anglican "apostate" George Whitefield were referred to frequently in the press and pulpit of eighteenth-century southeastern America, their prose writings are not to be met with nearly so frequently as the books by Tillotson and many of the other theologians, liberal and conservative, al-ready mentioned. Whitefield was prominently represented in the library at Bethesda and among the books of such clerical disciples as Baptist Isaac Chanler and Presbyterian-Inde-pendent Josiah Smith of Charleston. The North Carolina and Chesapeake New Lights, lay or clerical, do not seem to have preserved many (if any) of his sermons, journal, or tracts, though references indicate that they often had them.

Pietism, deism, and millennialism, among the many reli-gious features of eighteenth-century English thought, were also published and written about in America, perhaps more largely in the northern colonies but surprisingly often in the southeastern. The gazette presses in most of the southern provinces at times published books and pamphlets on religion, sometimes reprints of British treatises or sermons, sometimes locally originated material. By 1694 the Annapolis press was printing local sermons, and in 1700 it published commissary Bray's "inaugural" American sermon, "The Necessity of an Early Religion." Dozens more homilies, written by the clergy of that and neighboring provinces, appeared over the years, frequently on occasional topics of victory or defeat in war or for Masonic celebrations. In 1729 the Maryland press produced a Presbyterian catechism, an Anglican catechism, and a Church of England work on preparation for receiving the Lord's Supper.

The press in Charleston published even more religious

material, including a great deal of controversial matter that Maryland had largely avoided. Its first recorded offering was *A Dialogue between a Subscriber and a Non-Subscriber* in 1732, and at least two other reprinted religious works in the same year. In 1737 it had the honor of publishing the first edition of John Wesley's first hymnal, *A Collection of Psalms and Hymns,* which included several composed by the great churchman, then resident in Savannah. By 1740 the Charleston press was turning out pamphlets and sermons which were part of the Great Awakening and the Whitefield–Garden controversy, in both of which Harvard-educated local Presbyterian-Independent Josiah Smith was prominent. Smith was still championing Whitefield in print through the 1760s. Presbyterian cleric J. J. Zubly, of South Carolina and Georgia, in 1757 brought together *The Real Christian's Hope in Death,* possibly first issued by this press, and in 1759 it certainly issued a volume by Zubly's Anglican friend Richard Clarke. It did not publish the collected *Twenty Sermons* by Samuel Quincy, lecturer of St. Philip's in Charleston, which appeared from a Boston press.

The William Parks press at Williamsburg and its immediate successors tried to be impartial on religious questions, as the South Carolina press was. But as already noted, the Great Awakening received little direct attention in the form of books or pamphlets, though Samuel Davies's volume of verse is related to the great movement, and the controversy about the quality of that verse, occupying many pages of the *Virginia Gazette,* was certainly in large part a reflection of Anglican opposition to New Light evangelism. Most religious imprints in Williamsburg were reprintings of Church of England materials from Great Britain, such as Bishop Gibson's *The Sacrament* and two books of devotions in 1740, a volume by Leslie in 1733, and later books by Ussher (1736), Sherlock (1744), and Allestree (1746). There were original sermons or tracts by Anglican William Stith, Old Light Presbyterian John Caldwell, and New Light Samuel Davies in the 1740s, as well as Presbyterian John Thompson's *An Explanation of the Shorter Catechism* in 1749, among other American items. Perhaps most significant from the point of view of southern theological reading is the republication of three famous English works of the century. *The Whole Duty of Man* appeared in Williamsburg in 1746—one of its numerous reprintings; William Sherlock's *Practical Discourse Concerning Death* (1689) appeared in 1744 from the twentieth London edition—a perennial favorite throughout the southern colonies in all of the eighteenth century, almost rivaling *The Whole Duty of Man;* and the anti-Quaker polemicist Charles Leslie's *A Short and Easie Method with the Deists* . . . (1698) appeared from the fifth edition in 1733—a book considered by many orthodox Trinitarians the most effective brief answer to "scientific" religion.

Millennialism, so vital a part of Calvinism, especially in New England, that exponents of the Puritan origins of the American mind have labeled America "the redeemer nation," had its part in southern religious thinking. As in earlier British history, a belief in premillennial or postmillennial interpretation as proper for world (especially western European) history was by no means confined to Presbyterians or Puritans or Calvinists. Theologians of many varieties throughout the seventeenth and early eighteenth centuries expounded their concepts or used those of others for particular purposes. Ernest Tuveson makes a distinction between *millennialist* and *millenarian,* but most historians of ideas do not, and a distinction is not made here. In America, millenarianism really exploded in the Great Awakening—perhaps, as Alan Heimert believes, as a symptom of some colonials' dissatisfaction with the life of their time. A great part of it, however, as Tuveson has suggested, was a belief that the gospel was fleeing westward, a belief which assumed secular form in the conviction that human progress was destined to reach its climax in the New World.

Premillenarians believed that Christ's second coming would

immediately precede the millennium, or thousand years of holiness, in which Christ would rule the earth, and the post-millenarians that this second coming would follow this period. Jonathan Edwards's *History of the Work of Redemption*, for example, was postmillennial, a repudiation of the premillennialism of the preceding generation—confirmed for him by the revivals and the Great Awakening itself. He and other Calvinists saw, with George Whitefield, a glorious day was about to dawn. Samuel Davies saw the Seven Years' War as a contest which, by its outcome, might indicate whether the time was past or just come for the millennium. Unlike his New England contemporaries, Davies felt his oratorical powers inadequate to describe the majestic scene of the general resurrection, when the saints might overcrowd rather than inherit the earth. Many of his sermons, especially the patriotic exhortations, dwell on this theme. And it is a major element of his tract *Charity and Truth United* (c. 1755).

In South Carolina, Baptist parson Isaac Chanler's *The Doctrines of Glorious Grace Unfolded, Defended, and Practically Improved* (1744) brought in millennialism in defense of Whitefield and predestination and election. But Anglicans also were carried away by millennial (or millenarian) concepts, as was the Reverend Richard Clarke, successor to Alexander Garden as rector of St. Philip's in Charleston. Clarke, an eloquent and ecumenical theologian, prophesied in February 1759 that some great calamity would befall the city in September. He let his beard grow, at the same time running about the city and crying "Repent, Repent for the Kingdom of Heaven is at hand." His millenarian preaching must have been appealing, for he had a large following among the leading citizens. Two volumes of his *Sermons* and *A Second Warning to the World* were published in London in 1760. But by 1759 he had also brought out, in Charleston and in Boston, *The Prophetic Numbers of Daniel and John Calculated; In Order to shew the Time, When the Day of Judgment, For this first Age of the Gospel, is to be expected: And the Setting up the Millenial Kingdom of Jehovah and His Christ.* A subscriber to the *Sermons* was Henry Laurens, who sent a Moravian clergyman friend in North Carolina a copy of *Prophetic Numbers* in 1762 and discussed the book with him. The good and sensible Mr. Ettwein remarked:

As to Mr. Clark I wish he had remain'd a Preacher of Jesus Christ and think he would thereby have more wrought in the Vineyard of the Lord, than by his Writings. I know several blessed Servants of God, who have lost themselves in the Revelation Daniel; tho' I won't judge a Strange Servant. . . . Watch & pray for you know not when the Son of Man shall come, is argument enough for any Man to be prepared for the coming of the Lord.

As to his characterizing the Moravians, I can in Christian Love think no otherwise: but he did not know of whom he spoke nor what he wrote. Tho' it is true that we don't Spiritualize Religion & Sacred Things in that Way & Degree as he or the Quakers, yet if he had any better knowledge of the Brethren, than out of the writings of his & our Enemies, he could not have judg'd so.

The moderate Anglican Laurens almost surely agreed with his charitable friend.

Throughout the century psalms and hymns and music were a considerable part of southern religion, a fact which is reflected on the bookshelves. The standard Anglican psalters, such as Tate and Brady's 1696 *New Version of the Psalms of David*, began with Sternhold and Hopkins's 1562 version. Both were in southern libraries. But it is well to remember that Virginia treasurer George Sandys's *Paraphrase upon the Psalms of David* (1636) appeared in some eighteenth-century collections, and that during this period the Reverend Thomas Cradock of Maryland published, in Annapolis and London, *A New Version of the Psalms of David* (1754, 1756), and John Wesley in South Carolina his famous first *Collection of Psalms and Hymns* (1737) and Jonathan Badger *A Collection of the Best Psalm and Hymn Tunes* (1752)—all of which were in some southern libraries. There is no positive evidence that any of these American imprints were used in church services. "Wesley's Hymns" in some edition was for sale in the Lunenburg County Virginia store in 1797. Copies of the New England Bay Psalm Book were owned in Virginia and North Carolina, as was English John Playford's *Whole Book of Psalms* (9th 1707 ed.) in Virginia before 1778. In Virginia, plantation tutor Philip Fithian heard a full choir sing from its psalm books in 1774, and his employer, the planter–amateur musician Robert Carter of Nomini Hall, knew and played "Church tunes" and owned a considerable library of religious and other music. Presbyterian parson Samuel Davies was one of the two or three major American hymnodists of the eighteenth century. His verses were in British and American hymnals of most Protestant denominations from his own time into the early twentieth century. Davies's model was the great Isaac Watts, whose various editions of psalms and hymns were owned all over the South from not later than 1735 to the end of the century. Watts was popular with the laity of Anglican and dissenting persuasions.

Though the southern colonial and early nationalist owned theological volumes that were heavy with doctrine, including Calvinism and arguments for High Anglican and other involved doctrinal or liturgical positions, he advocated and usually practiced an unadorned, common-sense religion. William Byrd shows his mild orthodox rationalism more in his comment on the religious beliefs of Bearskin, his Indian guide on the Dividing Line expedition, than by his reading of Tillotson and other moderate divines. In 1720, writing to an English friend about the education of a child, opulent Robert "King" Carter neatly summarized the Anglican plain way:

Let others take what courses they please in the bringing up of their posterity, I resolve the principles of our holy religion shall be instilled into mine betimes; as I am of the Church of England way, so I desire they shall be. But the high-flown notions, and the great stress that is laid upon ceremonies, any farther than decency and conformity, are what I cannot come into the reason of. Practical godliness is the substance——these are but the shell.

In commissary James Blair's dedication of the 1722 edition of his widely read multi-volume collection of sermons, *Our Saviours Divine Sermon on the Mount . . . Explain'd and the Practice of It Recommended in Diverse Sermons and Discourses* (London, 1722; second edition 1740), the Virginia divine notes that in his colony he and his fellow clergy did not have to preach against deists, atheists, Arians, or Socinians, as in the m ther country: "Yet we find Work enough . . . to encounter the usual corruptions of Mankind, Ignorance, Inconsideration, practical Unbelief, Impatience, Impiety, Worldly-Mindedness, and other common Immoralities . . . the Practical Part of Religion being the chief Part of our Pastoral Care." It should be noted that even the eminent English dissenter Philip Doddridge commended Blair's sermons.

Like Blair, Presbyterian Davies had read widely and deeply in contemporary theology, including controversy, and in some of his sermons the dissenting pulpit writer, as a convinced Calvinist, gets into doctrinal matters. But as he repeated in his tracts and sermons from the English Chillingworth, "The Bible, the Bible is the religion of Protestants." This attitude, which southern American dissenters stressed, was certainly shared by the plainer or less educated Anglicans and was sympathized with by their more erudite brethren—unless rationalism had sunk too far into their approach to theology. Deeply oriented in the Bible was Hermon Husband of North Carolina, whose *Some Remarks on Religion* (Philadelphia, 1761) is an autobiographical account of a mystic's religious experience as he journeyed from Anglicanism to Whitefieldian Presbyterianism to Quakerism; it is worthy of comparison with Jonathan Edwards's *Personal Narrative*. Husband's little book is one of the significant pietistic works that emanated from and was owned and read in the South, though by no means the only one.

Thomas Jefferson, certainly not a sceptic but unitarian and rationalistic in his religious views, put together his personal Bible by clipping Christ's sayings from a copy of the New Testament. As he wrote a nephew, he believed that the Bible should be read as history, with the same questioning on the part of the reader to which he would submit any secular history he was studying. In his *Notes on the State of Virginia* he suggests that instead of putting the Bible or Testament into the hands of children whose judgments are not mature, their minds be stored first with ancient, modern European, and American history. He believed religion to be valuable primarily as it led to right conduct, a belief strongly suggestive of the earlier printed sermons of Blair and Jefferson's kinsman William Stith.

Thus two of the dominant religious currents of Britain and America were present in the beliefs and the reading of eighteenth-century southerners: pietism and rationalism. The southern rationalists almost disappeared with the Second Great Awakening at the end of the century and the beginning of the nineteenth, though they have remained a quiet minority among southern thinkers and writers on theology. They never included a majority of the upper classes. Of this group many remained orthodox Trinitarians. A sophisticated, sensitive, and successful industrialist such as Robert Carter of Nomini could never find the satisfying religion he craved in the Anglican or Episcopal church, and he wandered through various evangelical sects and ideas, including the Baptist and Swedenborgian, concerning which he read a great deal. He left the Baptists because of his dissatisfaction with Calvinist determinism, and he retained a rationalism he had learned from Voltaire. He seems to have died in a reasonably orthodox form of Arminianism.

All through the century southeasterners continued to read

and ponder sermons, usually the meditative or pious variety. Jane Ball of South Carolina, elegant and sophisticated mistress of a great plantation, read her Bible regularly, and occasionally a printed sermon sent to her by her son Isaac. In 1803 she requested that this son send her, from the family's town house, a copy of James Hervey's letters, a collection of religious and meditative epistles almost as popular in all the five southern states since about 1760 as the same author's *Meditations and Contemplations* (1745–1747). Pious and Calvinist and evangelical in sympathy, this book was a favorite of this good Anglican communicant of St. Philip's in Charleston.

The theological and religious reading of these southern eighteenth-century men and women, represented by the titles in their libraries and what they themselves wrote on Christianity, covers a fairly wide spectrum of belief and speculation. Sir John Randolph, Thomas Jefferson, and signer George Wythe were certainly liberal theologically. Their friends President James Madison and his cousin of the same name were moderate Trinitarians, and Edmund Pendleton was a strong religious conservative. The trenchant Virginia political polemicists Landon Carter and Richard Bland seem to have been as theologically orthodox as their major opponent the Reverend John Camm, and South Carolinian Henry Laurens was as orthodox a Trinitarian as any of the three. Scotch-Irish and other Presbyterians were of course Calvinists. Leading Baptists such as Elder John Leland or Andrew Broaddus or Isaac Chanler might be Calvinist or Arminian. It is perhaps more significant that in 1795 Broaddus published *The Age of Reason and Revelation* against "Mr. Thomas Paine's late piece."

There were a few men like the Appalachian Georgian blacksmith who took delight in shocking the simple backwoodsmen by reading and praising Tom Paine and Volney. But most artisans and small farmers, if they were religious at all, read the Bible, catechisms, and commentary ·emanating from dissenting—or, at the end of the century Methodist—sources. With the assistance of their evangelical clergy, they became or remained "convinced supernaturalists," expressing themselves most memorably in their great hymns.

The black, slave and free, was in this century, as far as we now know, also a convinced supernaturalist who expressed his hopes and aspirations in the oral artistry of his people, particularly in what we now call "spirituals," and in his hymns. Contrary to the wishes of many plantation masters and the sweeping statements of certain historians, a number of Negroes in every southern colony could read. Dr. Bray's Associates saw to the establishment of schools for them so that they might read the Bible, the Book of Common Prayer, and a catechism or two. The proportion who were literate dwindled rapidly between the end of the eighteenth century and the Civil War, but in the age of the American Revolution many native-born blacks were able to read and expound to their fellows. For them especially, among all southern class and ethnic groups, religious reading was a joy and an achievement.

Despite the impact of reason and deism as dominant intellectual theories of the age, the southern colonist of the eighteenth century, like his ancestors and descendants, usually remained a believer in revelation. Rationalism brought to New England a disintegration of a still rigid Puritanism into a Unitarianism among a large proportion of the body of churchgoing people. Despite scattered individual deists and some rough equivalent of the Unitarians, such a widespread disintegration never took place in the colonial South. The Anglican establishment and the Anglican doctrine had never been rigid, and religion had never occupied *the* central position in the southern mind. Even the Calvinism of Whitefield and the Presbyterians never came to dominate the lives of a great segment of the southeastern people. That is, it did not dominate to the exclusion of non-theological interests. The southern colonial might be reasonably devout, but he took his religion in stride. Its practice was a great reason but not the only reason for human existence.

THREE

Belles Lettres

WHEN THE TERM *LITERATURE* IS USED IN THE NARROW SENSE OF the body of writing that includes drama, poetry, fiction, criticism, and essays, and that continues to exist because of inherent imaginative and artistic qualities, it is frequently characterized as *belles lettres.* That is, it is the written expression of art for art's sake. But in any age it has been difficult to separate the purely artistic from the didactic or purposeful. Frequently the artistic form is employed to carry an obvious moral or political or social or religious lesson, as certain writings already cited so obviously do. And there are of course the borderline or double-purpose cases, of writings which are designed to teach and to entertain or delight at the same moment. From the classical critics such as Aristotle into our own time, there has been a preponderance of belief that the ultimate function of all art is morality or truth. A recent study of the American Enlightenment suggests that in its final stage, as it entered the nineteenth century, it had become the Didactic Enlightenment. To a certain extent, depending somewhat on definitions, it had always been that. But after 1800 the relation of beauty and truth might be ultimately the same in the writing of Wordsworth or Keats or the American Edgar Allan Poe.

For the eighteenth century of America in its southeastern region, there are some special emphases or qualifications to be noted or recalled. They are really western European or British, but they are reflected in the colony-states of our area with

additional qualities peculiar to the region. Though they have
already been noted, there should be a reminder here as one
considers the belletristic volumes on eighteenth-century southern shelves. First, in this age of reason everything, perhaps
especially including the printed word, was to be measured
according to its degree of usefulness. "Usefulness" was often
employed in the broad sense, and to many the giving of delight
or the stimulation to relatively unpractical cerebration was as
useful as the persuasion to goodness or instruction in politics
or technology or the subject matter of a learned profession.
One recalls, however, that the definition of the useful as anything which impels us toward an appreciation of beauty and
virtue may include (for the latter) much of what is now designated as the practical. Throughout the eighteenth century,
southern readers found that some novelists, such as Fielding,
for example, ridiculed the practical morality of Richardson's
Pamela. Joseph Addison, from the beginning to the end of the
century perhaps the most popular playwright (for one tragedy)
and essayist (particularly for the *Spectator*), wrote with politics
and morals and manners in mind, as well as aesthetic entertainment. Alexander Pope, the most popular poet, also included politics as well as manners and morals in his biting or
his gentler satires and gave a new moral tinge to Homer in his
great translations. Even Shakespeare, quite frequently found
in southern libraries and on the southern stage, too often
appeared in rationalized, sentimentalized, or overly moralized
versions by eighteenth-century playwrights who thought they
knew the temper of their age. Poems were written on the
advantages of growing indigo in South Carolina or sugar cane
in Jamaica, or on snakeroot or tobacco as cures for diseases.
Other plays than Addison's were written as political propa-
ganda, novels carried theories of education and a new social
order, and the familiar essay form was employed for a variety of
practical purposes.

Yet one should not, and indeed cannot, say that all the belletristic reading material of the period was in fact not that. Men and women did read for pleasure, for recreation, for sheer mental stimulus (if that ever exists alone), as the books on southern shelves, southern letters, and southern diaries indicate. As the century wore on, larger and larger proportions of the books advertised for sale, of the contents of public circulating or private social libraries, and of private, personal libraries were what one would even today call belletristic or at least recreational. Among them, the Greek and Latin classics, for example—a considerable part of the large and medium collections, which held their proportionate place until close to the end of the century—were certainly not all useful in the narrow sense. Among the Roman and Greek authors are some of the earliest writings the colonists knew devoted to humor—satiric or whimsical or jesting. In their libraries, aesthetic or literary criticism began chronologically with Aristotle and continued down to the critiques produced near the end of their own century, though some of it (such as Shaftesbury's) goes beyond the purely philosophical.

The southern settlers brought some belletristic or recreational books with them from the seventeenth into the eighteenth century. Many are directly or ultimately classical, from Greek or Latin originals of Ovid and Seneca and Horace (to mention only three of the most popular) or famous translations of these authors and others from the Renaissance or from Dryden. But by 1666 one planter had "a book called Lyons Play," and by the end of the century Beaumont and Fletcher and Ben Jonson were among the English playwrights represented. Aesop's *Fables,* destined to remain a favorite throughout the period to 1800, was in several mid-seventeenth-century inventories. Burton's *Anatomy of Melancholy* (which continued to be enjoyed by later southerners through William Gilmore Simms and Paul Hamilton Hayne) was in several libraries, and volumes of verse by Donne, Quarles, Herbert, and Waller were listed. Butler's *Hudibras* was in Virginia and North Carolina and almost surely Maryland and South Carolina before 1700. Cervantes's *Don Quixote* and several French romances joined Petronius's *Satyricon* as their prose fiction. Throughout the eighteenth century other belletristic works printed first in the seventeenth century or even earlier turn up in a number of southern libraries, and many of them undoubtedly were owned long before 1700, even though they fail to show in the fragmentary or carelessly laconic inventory entries.

Perhaps one of the distinctive features of eighteenth-century southern library inventories is the considerable amount of drama they contained. To the New World these relatively secular-minded settlers in the Southeast brought the taste for play-acting and plays which was so dominant a characteristic of English Renaissance men and women. Though Shakespeare was most frequently acted on the stage of the period, Ben Jonson and even Beaumont and Fletcher rival him on the bookshelves. Restoration and eighteenth-century playwrights are well represented in both places.

As far as is now known, the earliest copy of Shakespeare in British America appears in the 1699–1700 inventory of Virginia lawyer-planter Arthur Spicer as "Macbeth." The entry has been interpreted as referring to the 1673 quarto of that play. From then on, in all five southern colonies, "Shakespeare's Plays" or "Shakespeare's Works," sometimes with the addition of the name of the eighteenth-century editor or adapter, appears frequently. Rowe, Pope, Theobald, Boydell, and Hanmer are favorite versions, though there were editions by Capel and Samuel Johnson. In South Carolina, Edgar finds Shakespeare was the most popular literary author, and the known inventories for the other provinces would indicate that this was probably true from Maryland to Georgia. Any of the editions just mentioned would have been expensive, and usually would have been published in many volumes, and thus Shakespeare seems to have been rarer in the collections of men and women of moderate means than some of the special single-book authors who will be noted in a moment. Perhaps costliness may account for his curious absence from the libraries of most of the clergy. Many who possessed not only impressive collections of theology but numerous poets and other belletristic writers seem not to have owned Shakespeare, though at times they may quote him. He is often in the libraries of lawyers, planters, physicians, and public officials. Founding father Henry Laurens of South Carolina quotes *Henry VI, Part II* to imply that a local political placeman was a sly deceiver. Jefferson, who owned at least two multivolume eighteenth-century editions, does not make frequent reference to Shakespeare in his correspondence, but he speaks of *Macbeth* (Duncan's murder scene) approvingly, and a half-century later urges a study of all earlier English dialects as a proper approach to the beauties of "that divine poet." Sporadically through these fifty years he sought knowledge of an authentic portrait of the bard.

Since *Richard III*, the *Merchant of Venice, Othello, Romeo and Juliet, Hamlet, Henry IV, The Tempest*, and a half-dozen other plays were favorites on the southern stage in the eighteenth century, including the early national southern stage, it is probable that more persons owned copies of single plays, or even collected editions, than is now known. In the Maryland, Virginia, South Carolina, and Georgia gazettes the collected works were offered for sale until the end of the century, and the circulating private and commercial libraries contained them. For all these reasons it seems probable that there was widespread reading of Shakespeare in the upper and middle levels of society, at least after mid-century.

Publication and ownership of Shakespeare criticism in the

South is additional proof of the high value set upon his writings. Original essays on the quality and nature of his genius appear in the southern gazettes, and in the same newspapers were reprinted British commentary on his plays, such as Steele's *Tatler* No. 53 or Addison's *Spectator* Nos. 40 and 592. Mrs. Elizabeth Montagu's *An Essay on the Writings and Genius of Shakespeare compared with the Greek and French Dramatic Poets, with Some Remarks on the Misrepresentations of Mons. de Voltaire* (1769) was in private and circulating library collections from Maryland south in the last third of the century, and other critics better known through a longer portion of the century were represented over a correspondingly greater length of time.

Though Shakespeare was undoubtedly the most widely known and owned dramatic author, single plays or groups of plays by others were held in all the colonies. By any standard the most popular was Addison's tragedy *Cato*, already mentioned as a political piece, or so employed, but certainly appealing to readers and to audiences for a variety of qualities, including memorable characterization and dozens of eminently quotable lines. Published in 1713, it was owned in all five colonies by clergy, planters, frontiersmen, circulating lending libraries, and private society libraries. It was sold in 1750 at the bookstore in Williamsburg and advertised in the *Virginia Gazette* long before and after that date. In 1771 Jefferson recommended "Addison's plays" (principally Cato) for the basic library of his friend young Robert Skipwith. He probably knew that it had been produced in Williamsburg long before he was born, by 1736 at the latest. It appeared in a Baltimore theater in 1783. A Presbyterian, an Anglican, and a Methodist parson were among those who had it on their shelves. At least one of them, Samuel Davies, mentions it in a sermon.

William Byrd's friend William Congreve was well represented on southern bookshelves and in southern theaters for at least the latter two-thirds of the century. Again, he was owned in every colony: by a Maryland sheriff, a College of William and Mary president-clergyman-poet, a Virginia building contractor, physicians, merchants, planters, clergy, and at least two colonial governors. His *Works* was offered for sale in most of the gazettes' advertisements. In the 1730s one planter owned a single play, *Love for Love,* and years later *Animadversions on Congreve* was an item in a Virginia Custis family library. From the seventeenth century, Jonson, Beaumont and Fletcher, Aphra Behn, Thomas Shadwell, and Thomas Otway were among a dozen or two such items. Otway's *The Orphan* (1680) and *Venice Preserv'd* (1682) were perennial favorites on the southern stage to 1800, and they appear in at least two colonies on library or advertising lists. Aphra Behn, who had written a play and a novel with New World settings and themes, was on shelves in Virginia and North and South Carolina.

Probably all the better-known eighteenth-century playwrights were on some shelves in all five southern provinces, for their inhabitants, great or humble, enjoyed seeing stage productions and probably read the plays they saw before or after seeing them acted—as we know definitely some did and many still do. Extremely popular were the brisk semi-farces of Mrs. Susanna Centlivre, whose *Gamester, Busy Body, The Wonder: A Woman Keeps a Secret,* and *A Bold Stroke for a Wife* (all appearing between 1705 and 1737, with a collected *Works* in 1761–1762), in which her butts are the fine gentleman, the virtuoso, the trader, and the Quaker, were an anticipation of later drawing-room comedy. Copies of her plays were owned in Georgia and South Carolina and probably in the upper colonies. John Home's *Douglas* (c. 1756), an attraction on the boards throughout the latter half of the century, appears in libraries in Maryland, Virginia, and North Carolina. George Farquhar's *The Beaux' Stratagem: A Comedy* (1707) and *Recruiting Officer* (1706) were theater favorites throughout the century, and were owned in book form by such people as Maryland sheriff

Christie and by Thomas Jefferson. John Gay's *The Beggar's Opera* (1728), produced again and again in southern theaters to the end of the century, appears on the shelves in at least four of the colonies and to at least 1796. In 1732 William Byrd found a copy in backwoods Virginia which he read aloud on a rainy day, and he records that the "wit or humour that sparkled in it . . . killed the time, and triumphed over the bad weather."

One of the more interesting connections of the southern colonies with eighteenth-century British drama is the famous *The Careless Husband* (1704), almost universally attributed to poet laureate Colley Cibber. In the Huntington Library is a miscellaneous manuscript volume of original essays and verse by a Virginian of the third quarter of the century (now about to be published) in which is the story that William Byrd produced and acted in this play at an amateur presentation in the great hall of a mansion along the James, near his own, and that the master of Westover told the author of the anecdote that Byrd and two British noble friends were the actual authors of the play, which they had turned over to Cibber because they preferred anonymity. A recent essay on Byrd as poet and dramatist seems to confirm this claim, for verses in Byrd's manuscripts are songs in *The Careless Husband*. Amusingly enough, the great Presbyterian evangelist Samuel Davies, in the 1753–1754 diary of his journeys in England and Scotland, tells that one night in Newcastle-upon-Tyne, a city where he was unknown, he decided to satisfy a long-felt curiosity as to what acted drama was like. The play he saw was *The Careless Husband*! He commented only that "the Entertainment was short of my expectation." The printed version of this "entertainment," which he might have borrowed from Virginia neighbors, was also on the shelves in Maryland and South Carolina.

Steele's plays were fairly popular on the southern stage, and planters and physicians and libraries in several colonies owned printed copies. Sheridan was also a favorite on the American (including the southern) stage, but his dramatic works appear in few known southern inventories. Goldsmith, enormously popular in the late century, was probably represented dramatically on southern shelves by the collected works which Parson Weems sold so frequently and widely in the 1790s. Molière's plays were in the libraries in every colony, including those of Presbyterians and Anglicans, and a number of times in French, as in Mackenzie's collection in South Carolina and Jefferson's in Virginia. English adaptations of his comedies appeared in the southern theater in Maryland, Virginia, and South Carolina. The first Richmond playbill, of 1787, advertises his *The Cheats of Scapin*. Finally, on the shelves of a number of men who read and enjoyed drama was the most famous antidramatic criticism of the time, Jeremy Collyer's *A Short View of the Immorality and Profaneness of the English Stage* (1698). James St. John and Thomas Gadsden in South Carolina and William Byrd II and two Custises in Virginia were laymen who could appreciate Collyer's lively style and even his arguments when they did not agree with them, but one may be sure the Carolina Baptist parson Chanler and Maryland Presbyterian parson Taylor read *A Short View* with approbation.

Southern readers on the whole found the British drama a principal source of reading entertainment. In 1701 planter Ralph Wormeley had fifty comedies and tragedies in folio; in 1757 Sheriff Charles Christie owned collections of plays by Dryden, Farquhar, Otway, Congreve, Beaumont and Fletcher, and Cibber; in 1774 musician-industrialist Robert Carter of Nomini had the works of Farquhar, Wycherley, Shakespeare, Molière, Congreve, and Van Brugh; and in 1740 merchant Scot William Dunlop possessed one unidentified two-volume "Collection of Plays," Congreve in three volumes, Rowe in three, another collection of "Plays," and in French the tragedies of Corneille and the works of Racine. Several physicians and lawyers were among the dozens of others who gathered on their shelves the lively playwrights of their time and the age preceding. The records show that on rainy or winter days, such as Byrd described, families and friends gathered round fireplaces, assumed specific roles, and read aloud. In this recreation they differed quite distinctly from the contemporary "Saints" of New England, as Byrd loved to call the northeastern colonials.

→»»X««←

Even more popular and thus more often on southern shelves were the belletristic works from Greek and Roman antiquity. This was the golden age of classical antiquity in America, and much has been written recently on the ideas of republican government and society derived from the classical authors. Though Howard M. Jones, Clinton Rossiter, and Bernard Bailyn believe that educationally the study of the Graeco-Roman classics was only a gentleman's culture, they are in a distinct minority among intellectual historians. Anyone who went to school (and as already suggested, most did) began the learning process through Latin authors, unless he was an apprentice or a black. Though some prominent southern colonials, such as the Reverend James Maury, in time declared the classical education impractical, the same men continued to own and read and quote from those ancient literatures all their lives. Even artisan apprentices were likely to read and to quote from Aesop's *Fables* in translation.

The dramatists Plautus and Terence and Seneca, and Sophocles and Aeschylus and Euripides and Aristophanes, were in dozens of libraries. Wheeler finds Seneca the most popular classical author in Maryland (according to the inventories), though not necessarily entirely for his plays. Jefferson owned all of these playwrights in their original languages and in several editions of each, as did John Randolph of Roanoke. But the dramatists were never as popular as other poets, such as Ovid (first in frequency in Virginia) or Virgil (first in South

Carolina). Caesar's *Gallic War* (an elementary school text in the South through my boyhood) was referred to in terms indicating that every reader would know its content.

Aristotle and Horace, among other things familiar as advocates of the middle way in life, were probably quoted as epigraphs for essays or poems more than Cicero or Homer, though all four are in British and American reading material. And the satirists include Juvenal most frequently. The works of these authors and all the rest were owned in Maryland by merchants and clergy and lawyers and planters, many classics appearing in medium-size or small libraries.

Robert Morris, father of the founding father of that name and a rationalist, in his dying moments had his friend Henry Callister read Plato's *Phaedo* aloud to him. Morris is said to have found philosophical comfort in it. Jolly musician-parson Thomas Bacon ridiculed his attempts to give his sermons an air of profundity by quoting from or dressing up Virgil's thoughts as his own. And Annapolis lawyer Stephen Bordley advised his younger brother to study Cicero's letters if he wished to develop "a strong, nervous, artful way of writing and speaking."

The eighteenth century in Virginia was equally classical. These noted books and others are everywhere, from the 1696/1697 library of the Reverend Thomas Teackle on the Eastern Shore to Jefferson and Wythe and Randolph and Wirt. The urbane William Byrd had hundreds of classical volumes in his great collection, and he usually read them in the original languages. By general agreement Jefferson is considered the most perfect embodiment of the American Enlightment and "the advocate par excellence of the classics . . ., the last great humanist." But he had older and younger contemporaries who enjoyed Graeco-Roman belles lettres as much as he. One was his law teacher and fellow signer of the Declaration, George Wythe. Others were the learned Richard Bland and James Madison. A recent study, "The Latin Attainments of Colonel Landon Carter of Sabine Hall" (*Virginia Magazine of History and Biography* [1977], pp. 51–54), a large part of whose library still exists, concludes that the moody old revolutionist had read and mastered Roman literature and could quote and employ it from memory—"reassurance again of the knowledge and the spirit of the classics in colonial Virginia." This is part of an answer to a number of historians who have alleged that southern learning in Graeco-Roman literature was in general most superficial, and that Jefferson and Madison were "sports," or freakish deviations from the normal, in their knowledge.

On the enjoyment of the classics in the Chesapeake area, Jefferson should indeed have the last word, though he speaks for many more than himself: "To read the Latin and the Greek authors in their original is a sublime luxury; and I deem luxury in science to be at least as justifiable as in architecture, painting, gardening or the other arts. I enjoy Homer in his own language infinitely beyond Pope's translation of him . . ., and it is an innocent enjoyment. I thank on my knees him who directed my early education for having put into my possession this rich source of delight: and I would not exchange it for anything which I could then have acquired & have not since acquired." This was in 1800. Some eleven years earlier he had written: "But as we advance in life . . . things fall off one by one, and I suspect we are left with Homer and Virgil, perhaps with Homer alone." Even before 1789 he was attempting to make a complete collection of the Greek authors.

In the two Carolinas there is record of the classics on the shelves of parish or personal libraries from 1700. In South Carolina in private collections Horace was almost as frequent as Virgil, and Plutarch and Cicero and Homer and Juvenal and Persius are among the other authors recorded. In Georgia, Burrington had Horace, Seneca, Cato, Vergil, Ovid, and Cornelius Nepos in 1767. A 1790 Savannah bookstore offered Cicero, Plutarch (in translation), Eutropius, and Pliny—not a great proportion in a long, four-column list. The large Georgia libraries described generally by De Brahm and Muhlenberg certainly contained many more.

Perhaps surviving from seventeenth-century colonial libraries but probably as frequently bought in the eighteenth century, as by Byrd and Jefferson and Laurens and Mackenzie, were dozens of early English authors. North Carolina Governor Arthur Dobbs, Virginian William Byrd, South Carolinian John Mackenzie, Virginian Godfrey Pole, Maryland parson Samuel Skippon, and others owned editions of Chaucer. The *Virginia Gazette* bookstore in 1755 offered Ogle's eighteenth-century edition. Jefferson had a 1598 black-letter edition (the so-called Lydgate-Speght version), the 1721 John Urry edition, and the 1741 George Ogle modernization. Jefferson also had a 1550 black-letter version of William Langland's *The Vision of Pierce Plowman*, a copy he bought from Professor Samuel Henley in 1785. Numbers of southerners in four colonies had Spenser's *Works* or his *Faerie Queene*, and this author was also advertised for sale in Williamsburg in 1755—almost surely indicative of some demand. Michael Drayton, George Sandys, Sir Philip Sidney, Geoffrey of Monmouth, Roger Bacon, and probably John Gower are in various inventories from Maryland to South Carolina, usually in eighteenth-century editions. William Byrd's library list includes the tantalizing item "Caxton's History of Troy," the original edition of which appeared between 1471 and 1476, and Ralph Wormeley's earlier collection has the enigmatic "Gower de" (John Gower?).

Foreign titles, often but not always in English translation, are also found. Castiglione's *The Book of the Courtier* in Sir Thomas Hoby's translation was in at least three Virginia collections, and Camoen's *Lusiad* in Mickle's English version was in as many Maryland libraries. Boileau, Dante, Descartes, Marmontel, Rabelais, and Quevedo y Villegas were in at least three libraries, and most of them in at least three colonies. Cervantes, Fénelon, Fontenelle, Erasmus, Le Sage, Montaigne, and Boccalini, in the original French, Spanish, Italian, or in English, are usually found in all five colonies. George Sale's translation of the Koran, with its famous "Preliminary Discourse" (to which Poe was indebted in many of his poems and

tales), was read in Maryland in 1742 by lawyer Stephen Bordley, who found it "an ingenious performance." Virginians
and South Carolinians also bought it. Rousseau, Spinoza, and
Voltaire appear on the shelves of a number of late-century
southerners. One North Carolinian owned fifty books in
French, a South Carolinian eighty, and some Virginians, including Carter of Nomini and Jefferson, as many or more than
the Carolinians. Perhaps almost a dozen modern languages are
represented in the collections of Byrd and Jefferson and some
of the large Georgia libraries mentioned by De Brahm, though
of the last there remain few lists of titles. Curiously, German
literature, except in the theological collections of the Salzburg-
ers and Moravians, is unrecorded. Surely the waves of German
immigrants in Charleston brought more books than the purely
theological, and so must the north Europeans who spread from
Pennsylvania down the Valley of Virginia.

Sources for some later forms and examples of southern humor
may have existed at least in part in private and even public
libraries. Usually but not always strongly flavored with the
satiric, books designed to provoke laughter were in seventeenth-century private libraries. Richard Lee (d. 1715) had a
1661 edition of *Wit and Drollery,* a volume of verse, and a 1648
Nugae venales, a jestbook. *Wit's Commonwealth* and *Pitts to
Purge Melancholy* were owned by early planters, and Jefferson
had *The Muse in Good Humour; or, A Collection of Comic
Tales,* as well as the classic humorists such as Cervantes,
Rabelais, and Laurence Sterne. Joe Miller's jests, rejuvenated
in nineteenth-century America through minstrel shows, were
offered for sale several times in Georgia between 1763 and 1790,
as were Falstaff's and Tom Brown's jests. Tom Brown ("of
facetious memory") was on the shelves of the Charleston Li-

brary Society before 1770. The tall tale related by John Lawson
in North Carolina by 1709 and the gusto and earthiness and
conscious interest in humor shown in the writings of the
southern George Alsop, Ebenezer Cook, William Byrd, and the
author of *"Dinwiddianae"* may have sprung at least as much
from oral tradition as from the written word, but these men
knew their jestbooks. The scatalogical verse-narrative, still
written at the end of the century by dignified St. George
Tucker, represented an English tradition that goes back beyond Chaucer and was popular in the eighteenth century, but as
it appears in the southern gazettes before Tucker, it suggests a
combination of influences from what men read and what they
heard. William Byrd seems to testify to double sources of
humor, the oral portion deriving in part from southern colonial ways of living, in his "Secret History of the Dividing
Line."

Verse appears in even the small southern libraries, varying in
form and purpose from the Hudibrastic satire, through the
nonclassical pastorals and odes, to the emotional hymns and
preromantic expressions of the sublime and melancholy in
natural beauty. As satire, it was perhaps most often a vehicle
for the political or didactic, though certain graces of meter and
imagery have given it a place in belles lettres. The mock-epic
frequently became, as in Pope's *Rape of the Lock,* preemi-
nently a work of art, despite whatever didactic intent existed in
its creation. The southern colonial had most or all varieties of
poets and poems on his shelves, and when he himself sat down
to indite, usually composed in the forms of Butler or Dryden or
Quarles or other versifiers still popular in the Britain of his
time, or in obviously more direct imitation of his Anglo-
Scottish contemporaries.

Not only were Chaucer and the Elizabethans (usually in eighteenth-century editions) present, but favorites from the preceding century, such as George Herbert, John Oldham, Francis Quarles, the earl of Rochester, and Edmund Waller. Milton's verse, reprinted often, was owned in every southern colony, though the first recorded copy (outside New England in America) is in 1716 in the library of Virginian Godfrey Pole. Curiously the so-called Cavalier poets, Herrick, Suckling, Lovelace, and Carew, are rare indeed in the secular eighteenth-century South, and there is no evidence that they were popular earlier. Dryden, like Milton, was represented everywhere for his verse as well as his other writings. Despite Quarles's Puritan sobriety, and perhaps because of his mingled Puritan and Catholic religiosity or the appeal of his adaptations of Alciati's emblems to English tastes, his *Emblems* (1635), *The Shepard's Oracles* (1646), and *Enchiridion* (1640–1641) appear in southern collections a number of times, from Wormeley's in 1701 to George Washington's in 1799. Edmund Waller was owned in at least three colonies and was offered for sale in new editions at least as late as 1772. That he appears most frequently in Virginia inventories may be because the Waller family of that colony believed themselves to be his collateral descendants.

But of all seventeenth-century English poets, Samuel Butler with his *Hudibras* (1663–1678) was by far the most popular. Though only the learned reader is likely to know him today, his *Hudibras* was written to appeal to "the robust parsons and lawyers and country squires who welcomed the poem with bellows of happy laughter." They understood its allusions to men and sects and Calvinism and Covenant, and their southern counterparts did too. But though it is awkward and clumsy, besides its polemical purpose it has aesthetic value. It entertains and amuses, and its verses give the impression that the spontaneous and fortuitous as well as the purposive and foreseen are present. The book, often in Zachary Grey's 1744 edition, is found in dozens of inventories in all five colonies in

the latter half of the century. It was still offered by the booksellers at least as late as 1790, and it was bought by all sorts of
people, including clergymen. Essays in colonial newspapers
refer to and quote from it (see the *South-Carolina Gazette,*
June 30–July 7, 1732) and southern colonial poets, from Marylander Ebenezer Cook in 1708 to the American Revolutionary
polemicists, employ its meter and some of its imagery. In 1769,
James Reid of King William County in Virginia quoted from
it in his social satire. William Byrd in September 1770 recorded
in his diary that he was reading Butler's *Hudibras,* a copy of
which the governor had just presented to him. Byrd refers to
the work twice in his "History of the Dividing Line," noting
that the chaplain of the expedition was annoyed at the survey-
or's reading the poem aloud, and comparing a lean deer to
Hudibras's horse, which "had hardly flesh enough to cover its
bones." There can be no doubt that the southern planter found
the work highly entertaining.

The second most popular early poet was John Milton,
whose verse does not appear in southern inventories until 1716.
The major epics may have been in the South in the century in
which they were written, as in New England; the prose certainly was. But *Paradise Lost* was on Virginian Alexander
Spotswood's shelves before 1726, and thereafter this great epic
and *Paradise Regained* seem to have stood side by side in
dozens of southern libraries. By 1728 Maryland poet Richard
Lewis refers in his *Muscipula* to something from Milton.
Welsh Virginia poet and Anglican priest Goronwy Owen in
1770 had Milton's *Poems* in two volumes, and Presbyterian
Virginia parson Samuel Davies quotes lines from *Paradise
Lost* in his sermons, and his verse owes something to Milton's
meters and imagery (though not nearly so much as it owes to
George Herbert). But editions of *Poems* or *Paradise Lost* and
Paradise Regained appear on the shelves of lawyers, planters,
schoolmasters, clergy, physicians, and merchants in all five
southern provinces. The two principal studies of Milton in

early America ignore almost completely the presence of this poet in the early south Atlantic area, and therefore nothing seems to have been done to determine his place in the region's colonial mind and art. All there is space for here is this notice that his verse was in dozens of private libraries, and that he was frequently referred to or quoted in the southern gazettes from 1732 to 1800.

English poets of the eighteenth century were bought by hundreds of their colonial contemporaries. Blackmore, Congreve, Cowper, Dyer, Dr. Garth, Glover, Goldsmith, Hill, Parnell, Pomfret, and Prior—all except Cowper and Goldsmith now almost completely forgotten save by the scholar—were owned in several instances in each of the five provinces. Matthew Prior, slightly whimsical, patriotic, and writing of "life as it is daily lived," appealed to merchants and planters and professional people in Virginia and the Carolinas from 1726 to the end of the century. John Gay's poems (other than his musical dramas or fables) were in all five colonies from not later than the 1730s to 1776. But for his own English generation and for southern Americans, his *Fables* was his most important work. Light and genial, it is still readable. Scottish Allan Ramsay, who includes verses in the preface to his *Tea-Table Miscellany* by his friend the Virginia physician Mark Bannerman, is represented on the shelves of every southern colony, including Georgia.

Not surprisingly the great characterisitc and favorite poet of Great Britain throughout the latter three quarters of the century, Alexander Pope, was owned, quoted, and imitated throughout the colonies from Maryland to Georgia. His prestige in all America was enormous, but his biting wit, apparently genuine religious devotion, and integrity of character, combined with his polished, complete, and elaborate if stylized imagery, made him the "Heaven-Taught Bard" for all kinds of southern colonials. Almost no southern poet escaped his influence, including Samuel Davies and William Dawson and James Sterling and James Kirkpatrick; the latter two addressed laudatory or elegiac verses to him from Maryland and South Carolina. In epigraphs for introducing newspaper essays on any subject, his couplets appear hundreds of times. The *Essay on Man,* the *Dunciad,* the *Essay on Criticism,* the *Iliad* and the *Odyssey,* the *Satires,* and the miscellanies and collected works were on the shelves of all sorts of people, from a half-dozen governors to sheriffs, merchants, physicians, building contractors, and revolutionaries. His works were still for sale in 1797 in the Lunenburg County Virginia country store, and he continued to be quoted frequently for another half-century. Pope was a Tory, but his works stood side by side with those of the great English Whigs on the shelves of Charles Carroll of Carrollton, Richard Bland, Landon Carter, George Washington, Thomas Burke, and a dozen other southern libertarians just before, during, or just after the Revolution. Quite clearly he was not read for his party politics, but just as clearly these southern movers for independence shared some of his conservative points of view. Largely they read Pope for his manners and morals and sound good sense, for his probing or slashing humor, certainly for what was for them his felicity of expression, and for a variety of charming tales in meter. A couplet of his might open an issue in a prose essay, as in the *Virginia Gazette* of September 29, 1752. It is worth noting that the same two lines appeared on the tombstone of a South Carolina plantation overseer about 1800:

> A Wit's a Feather, and a Chief a Rod,
> An honest Man's the noblest Work of God.

Then too, his religious poems (e.g., "The Dying Christian to

His Soul") gave a sense of comfort. In tribute a few months after his death a colonial wrote what most men felt (*South-Carolina Gazette,* June 17, 1745):

> This is thy Praise, due from every Pen,
> The greatest poet and the best of men.

But aesthetic and literary tastes were changing even as Pope died. The great dissenting evangelism of the Whitefields and Wesleys and Wattses produced in Britain, almost as a by-product, the moving verses that today are in almost every Protestant hymnal (as has been noticed briefly under "religion"). A product of the new sublimity of Shaftesbury and his successors and a shaper of their ideas, the songs and hymns in their emotional and transcendent Christianity led readers and thinkers away from a reliance on reason toward intuition and imagination and fancy. As already noted, Wesley and Samuel Davies contributed to this form of song in the southeastern colonies, where both were first published. It is not far from this religious verse to their purely belletristic verse, especially in Watts and Davies.

The never-dying poetic interest in nature in all its forms, but especially in natural landscape, was strongly reasserting itself in new and old meters and imagery in England by the 1730s. James Thomson, whose *Castle of Indolence: an Allegorical Poem Written in Imitation of Spenser* was published in 1748, had by 1730 established himself as a popular poet with the separate and collected version of *The Seasons.* Sentimentality, Shaftesburian optimism, blank verse instead of heroic couplets, natural description employed to assert philosophically the courses of things, and exaltation of nature as a great and serious subject are among the qualities which made *The Seasons* a popular poem in all of Britain and mark it as a great step away from neoclassicism. It is found in southern colonial libraries from at least 1740, and in all five provinces. Purcell found it enormously popular in North Carolina: in one instance it was the only belletristic work in a 1748 library of more than 204 titles. It was offered for sale in lists of the 1760s and 1770s and in public and private circulating libraries in the same periods in Maryland and Georgia. Jefferson had it in a separate edition and in the collected *Works* of 1744. Samuel Davies often quoted from it in his sermons. The *Works* is listed in at least a dozen inventories, though the separate title is more frequent. Thomson's lesser-known long poem, *Liberty*, published in five parts in 1735–1736 and complete in 1738, suggesting the familiar Whig history going back to the Saxons (as depicted by Tacitus), is not known as a separate title on southern shelves. The colonial southerner, as an out-of-doorsman, may have enjoyed *The Seasons* for its depiction of, or at least reaction to, physical environment, but its form and novel imagery and libertarian philosophy may also have attracted him.

Even more popular than Thomson—to judge again from the extent of inventories and frequent allusion or quotation—was Edward Young, whose major poem *Night Thoughts* (1742–1746) was in its century the best-known work of the so-called preromantic graveyard school of poets. Not bad in small doses, it was translated in full into all the major European languages. As Howard Mumford Jones drily remarks, like other mediocre literary things it translates well. Young's poetical *Works* was available in many collections, but it is this one poem which is quoted most often. Scottish James Reid, tutor in Virginia, uses lines from *Night Thoughts* in his prose satire on the religion and the society of the county in which he lived. Much earlier Samuel Davies had dozens of times quoted this poet of death and eschatology in his sermons and in his theological tracts. He once commented that "of all the poetical Pieces I ever read, the Night thoughts, I think have been most serviceable to me; and I shall keep them as my companion, till I commence an Immortal." William Byrd II, who tried unsuccessfully to secure as his second wife the London heiress who later married Young, seems not to have been interested in his successful rival's earlier poetry, and *Night Thoughts* was too late for the master of Westover. From 1740 at latest, Young's *Works* was in private libraries, from the largest collections to the small one of Mrs. Margaret Akins of South Carolina in 1757. The platitudinous "pleasurable melancholy" must have appealed to readers of the gazettes, for selections or brief quotations from the poem were printed into the nineteenth century. In 1806, Chesapeake lawyer and man-of-letters William Wirt tried to buy a copy from the Ralph Wormeley estate catalogue. In one poem at least, a generation later Edgar Allan Poe seems to be echoing a line from *Night Thoughts,* and the verses by Young were used extensively by Poe's friend the Georgian Thomas Holley Chivers.

Though Cowper's *The Task,* Goldsmith's *The Deserted Village,* and the poems of Burns were in some southern libraries by the 1790s, they were not popular in the South until the next century. Samuel Johnson in prose and verse is found in the age of Jefferson (after 1800) but rarely before, except for the *Rambler.* Macpherson's Ossian was a favorite of Jefferson and Bishop James Madison in the eighteenth century. St. George Tucker, himself a poet, had Young and Collins and Gray but appears not to have known his younger romantic contemporaries, or even Blake or Cowper. If this was a cultural lag, it was shared by rural Britain and the Yale Poets and Philip Freneau.

One may speculate, however, that it represents the usual reading tastes throughout the English-speaking world.

American-composed verse was surprisingly well known even outside the colony or area in which it originated. From the early eighteenth century, Virginian John Fox's *Mottos of the Wanderers,* a London publication, was owned by a fellow colonist and student at Trinity College, Cambridge, and by William Byrd. Richard Lewis's *Muscipula* (1728), a translation-adaptation of Holdsworth's Latin poem by a Marylander, appears in some early inventories, as does William Dawson's *Poems on Several Occasions by a Gentleman of Virginia.* Davies's *Miscellaneous Poems* (1751–1752) was almost a best seller, at least in the Chesapeake area. And poems by North Carolinian Thomas Godfrey, South Carolinian James Kirkpatrick, and Marylanders Ebenezer Cook and Thomas Cradock appear in the inventories. Perhaps even more interesting, for it suggests inter-colonial communication, are volumes of verse by Joel Barlow, Timothy Dwight, John Trumbull, Phillis Wheatley, David Humphreys, Joseph Hopkinson, and Philip Freneau. Richard Lee in 1715 owned Philip Pain's little 1668 volume of religious poems, published in Cambridge, Massachusetts, and now known in a presumably unique contemporary copy. Jefferson had some of these and others, such as St. George Tucker's *Probationary Odes* of 1786 and Mercy Otis Warren's *Poems* of 1790.

The nonfictional belletristic prose on southern shelves was most often the essay, in periodical or single or collected form. And it usually appeared in the English periodical, of which the

Spectator is overwhelmingly the most frequent example. There are more than three times as many collected editions of this work of Addison and Steele in South Carolina inventories, for example, as of Shakespeare, the most popular purely belletristic item. Next to it are the *Guardian* and *Tatler,* also by Addison and/or Steele. All three were in collected editions before the end of the second decade of the eighteenth century. Addison also wrote for the *Free-holder* (1715–1716) and the *Old Whig* (1719), and Steele for other periodical series. In the *Virginia Gazette* Dr. Samuel Johnson's the *Rambler* was most frequently drawn from for reprinted essays, primarily in 1751–1752, immediately after its first appearance. Other periodical essay collections, such as the *Craftsman,* the *Idler,* the *Rambler,* the *British Apollo,* and files of *Gentleman's* and *London* and *Scot's* magazines, are listed as bound volumes. There were dozens of others.

In southern collections the *Spectator* is almost as likely to be present as the Bible. Outside South Carolina it appeared on scores of shelves in Maryland, Virginia, North Carolina, and Georgia. Like Benjamin Franklin, many southern founding fathers learned to write good prose by using its essays as models. The *Tatler* and *Spectator* particularly were models for the earliest essays in the *Virginia Gazette,* the "Monitor" series. These and other British essay serials determined the form of most non-news items in the Maryland and the South Carolina gazettes. James Madison and William Byrd praised the *Spectator* essay as a proper guide for youth, and as late as 1803 Attorney General William Wirt declared the Addisonian prose piece to be the appropriate model for literature designed to educate a young America. But one should not believe that the periodical essay was read solely or even primarily for its moral or social lessons. It was usually a graceful, entertaining presentation of any sort of subject, including the place of the country gentleman in contemporary society. Sir Roger de Coverley was easy to identify with the southern planter. And the pieces on witchcraft, antiquity, music, painting, and the Orient, as well as those on manners and morals, were all concerned with matters in which he was interested.

The periodical essays included a great deal on theories of art and education, of beauty and truth, of criticism of drama and epic poetry, of the function of all poetry, of fancy and the imagination. But these subjects were discussed in more detail in incisive analytical discourses that were printed as pamphlets or books. As a recent perceptive critic has pointed out, though no indigenous philosophy was developed in colonial America (with the possible exception of Jonathan Edwards's thought), there was philosophy and some philosophical thinking before 1776. Jefferson may have done some of this philosophical thinking, not only in religion and politics but in literature and aesthetics generally, but he developed no original ideas or thought patterns, according to this critic. Perhaps so. Jefferson himself was the first to claim he never intended to do so. But for this reader the published and unpublished comments on a rationale of religion expressed by Arthur Dobbs and Samuel Davies and William Byrd and the economic-political cogitations of John Taylor of Caroline were well formed by 1800 and at least lead to more fully developed philosophies, such as those of Edmund Ruffin and John C. Calhoun.

There were in colonial southern libraries a considerable number of volumes of literary criticism, aesthetics, or other forms of philosophy which their owners almost surely read, even though they developed no principles from them. Many library shelves held Aristotle's *Poetics* and *Ethics,* and proof that they were read lies in the many allusions to them in southern newspaper essays. Similarly the colonials possessed and quoted Horace's *Art of Poetry* and Longinus's *On the Sublime.* As noted in the discussion of political theory, Shaftesbury's *Characteristics* was enormously popular in the Southeast. It included studies of aesthetics and literary crircism, among them the famous "Inquiry Concerning Virtue or Merit," written not later than 1700. Its theories of taste, innate goodness, the nature of the sublime and of beauty, and other "romantic" ideas were later to affect profoundly the whole course of British and European art and theory of art. His ideas are reflected, directly or indirectly, in the writing of Samuel Davies and Thomas Jefferson (of which more in a moment). Many shelves in the two Chesapeake colonies and the Carolinas held Edward Bysshe's *Art of English Poetry* (1702), a simple manual of prosody with a rhyming dictionary, perhaps the best known of such contemporary volumes, for in Hogarth's engraving, "The Distressed Poet" (1735), it lies before the distraught rhymester. Prose polemicist Landon Carter, who evidently exchanged versified epistles with his crony "Dick" (Richard) Bland, owned the seventh edition of 1725, which still stands in the Sabine Hall library beside a volume titled *A Discourse upon Epick Poetry*. A number of colonials owned, in French or English, the critical essays of Boileau and Rapin and Rollin (and Rollin's *Method of Studying the Belles Lettres*). The Charleston Library Society had several other studies in criticism in French or by French authors. The Anglo-French Andrew Michael Ramsay, whose *Travels of Cyrus* was fairly common in the southern colonies, had prefixed "Discourse on Epic Poetry" to the 1717 Paris edition of Fénelon's *Télémaque,* and it found its way into our early libraries in both languages.

William Hogarth's *Analysis of Beauty* (1754) was also available. And in the latter part of the century Henry Home, Lord Kames's *Elements of Criticism* (1762), and Francis Hutcheson's *An Inquiry into the Original of Our Ideas of Beauty and Virtue* (1725) appeared on many southern shelves. Kames's work and Hugh Blair's *Lectures on Rhetoric and Belles-Lettres* were reprinted more than thirty times each in America and Britain and were used as school and college texts well into the nineteenth century.

From these critical volumes, or with their aid, Samuel Davies formed his theory of the form and function of poetry which he expressed in the introduction to his mid-century volume *Miscellaneous Poems*. We know that he owned Aristotle on poetry, for the record of his purchase still exists in the ledgers of the Williamsburg bookstore. And that many other readers were interested in aesthetic theory is evidenced not only by the allusions just noted but by reprinted and original essays on the subject in the southern gazettes to the end of the century.

Though it is not easy to identify the basis of Thomas Jefferson's literary ideas or to label his poetic theory, a recent scholar made a good beginning in an essay published in 1977. Jefferson received the ideas most congenial to him from the ancients. The words *sublimity* or *sublime,* his most frequent critical terms to describe art or nature, may have come from Longinus and Shaftesbury. He seems to reserve his highest praise for "literature which expresses rational truth in a lucid but affecting manner." That is, literature should present a rationalistic sublimity. Though he has often been labeled a hopelessly old-fashioned neoclassical critic, on closer examination he appears to be in his early writing, with Edmund Burke and James Macpherson (Ossian was his delight), an anticipator or practitioner of preromantic Gothicism, and he set precedents by striving in his prose to render political ideas with strongly emotional effects. Before 1800, he and other southern men and women were combining their reading and taste, shaped by experience, into aesthetic theory.

The rhetorical-oratorical side of this theory in books in southern libraries has been noted only indirectly. Demosthenes and Quintilian, and Cicero and Lycurgus and Peter Ramus were well represented among their books, as were several eighteenth-century writers on the art of preaching or elocution or eloquence, such as David Fordyce and Sheridan. Hugh

Blair also was influential. The continuity of interest in the theory and practice of oral rhetoric carried through the nineteenth century in the South, perhaps beginning with William Wirt and James Ogilvie in 1802–1803.

Allied to all this are John Locke's *Essay Concerning Human Understanding* (1690), throughout the century everywhere in the Southeast, as well as the rest of America; the more generally philosophical works of Descartes and Hutcheson; and the end-of-the-century Rousseau and the Scottish Common-Sense school. Jefferson had scores of their writings, and they are in public and private circulating libraries and individual collections during the latter half of the century.

Prose satire of many kinds—the dialect letter, the tongue-in-cheek essay, the brief and the long narrative—was well represented. The major author who employed it in a variety of ways, Dean Jonathan Swift, was present in *Miscellanies* and collected *Works,* but especially in *Gulliver's Travels* and *A Tale of a Tub.* Not later than the 1730s he was in every colony, read by Anglican and dissenting clergy, several governors, a sheriff, merchants, physicians, and many others, including Jefferson and Washington. Jefferson was one of several who owned the earl of Orrery's "Life of Swift," as it was usually designated. The *Tale* may have been read as a fable or a religious tract, but its richness goes beyond those elements, as writers in southern newspapers realized. *Gulliver's Travels* began in 1713–1714 as an attack on pedantry in the form of voyages. But it became the most seriously pondered and most complex of all his works, a book of Christian pessimism which sees man as a fallen creature. It is a book in which the Anglo-Irish and the Scotch-Irish in the southern American colonies might see Ireland's and mankind's plight. And all colonials might enjoy it, in this age of reason through satire, for the imaginative qualities with which reason and satire were combined. It was an entertaining grotesque narrative for the young colonial, but one has only to read southern newspapers to realize that the more mature saw in it what Swift had meant they should.

Fiction in prose form was relatively rare on southern shelves in the first half of the century. A few novels by Mrs. Aphra Behn and the French women of the seventeenth century were scattered here and there, and more rarely Sir Philip Sidney's *Arcadia.* Cervantes was indeed an exception, popular in translation before 1700 and continuing to 1800. In the early period Defoe's *Robinson Crusoe* and *Works* were occasionally present, along with Le Sage's novels in French or English. The rogue literature then popular in London, a form to which Defoe contributed in some of his best-known fiction, was rarely recorded in southern inventories, though one William and Mary professor wrote several novelettes in the form. Byrd's large library catalogue lists very few English novels, and even those few, such as *Tom Jones,* were added to the Westover collection after his death.

With the publication of Richardson's *Pamela* in 1740 and his other novels of character, and those of Fielding, Smollett, and Sterne in the next twenty years, as well as the subsequent deluge of imitations and the Gothic, sentimental, and Oriental fiction of the rest of the century, the matter and degree of recreational reading changed markedly, and in no place more than in the later eighteenth-century South. The fragmentary ledger of the *Virginia Gazette* bookstore for 1751–1752 and 1764–1765 indicates something of the changing tastes. From the classical and religious books sold in the earlier period, the customers—governors and farmers and schoolboys—were turning to the recreational reading, and especially to prose fiction. In neither period were Virginians great purchasers of Richardson's three novels, perhaps because they agreed with Fielding that it was monstrous that Pamela's "virtue" had to be rewarded. Richardson appears to have been more popular to the north, including the Boston area, and Benjamin Franklin's 1744 edition of *Pamela* was the first novel published in America. But Virginians bought the first six volumes of Sterne's *Tristram Shandy* before the work had been completed, and the seventh and eighth volumes were sold in Williamsburg in the same years in which they were issued. In the early nineteenth century *Tristram Shandy* and *A Sentimental Journey* were still referred to and quoted in correspondence and even courtrooms throughout the coastal South. Fielding, too, was a better seller than Richardson, and Smollett was favored even more by Chesapeake readers.

There were copies of Richardson, however, in all five southern provinces before 1763. The Reverend Thomas Bacon of Maryland, in returning to a merchant friend his copy of *Clarissa Harlowe,* thanked him in verse:

> I've sent your Miss Clarissa Harlot,
> Pox take me for a Blundering Varlet!
> Harlow, I mean in Seven Books,
> Of Pyeous Use for Pastry Cooks;
> To Captain Hoper's I have sent them,
> With thanks from those to whom you lent them. . . .

In 1763 the *Georgia Gazette* advertised that *Pamela* and *Sir Charles Grandison* were for sale, and both the Virginia and the Maryland gazette offered Richardson, among other novelists. Eliza Lucas Pinckney of South Carolina was reading them soon after they were published in Great Britain, though Charlestonians may have had Franklin's Philadelphia edition of *Pamela.* They are recorded in a dozen or so pre-Revolutionary private libraries, including five in South Carolina that had

Clarissa Harlowe. In 1790 in Savannah both *Clarissa* and *Sir Charles Grandison* were offered for sale.

Fielding's *Tom Jones* rivaled or exceeded Sterne's *Tristram Shandy* in popularity throughout the latter half of the century, and *Joseph Andrews* was in many private collections. *Amelia* and *Tom Jones* were advertised by the Savannah bookstore in 1790, in the *Georgia Gazette* in 1763, and in the *Virginia Gazette* in 1755. Lord Botetourt, George Washington, Eleazar Allen, Dr. John Eustace, parson Thomas Bacon, and Robert Morris were among those who had one or more of Fielding's novels on their shelves. Sterne's fiction was acquired in fine editions by Thomas Jefferson when he was in Europe in the 1780s, and it was then that he commented to his nephew Peter Carr that "the writings of Sterne particularly form the best course of morality that ever was written." Perhaps many of his contemporaries agreed with him, but others certainly read it for the double entendres, leering obscenity, sentimentality, and whimsical humor of the work.

Smollett's ability to combine realistic characterization with picaresque narrative was one of the qualities which made his five major narratives (published between 1748 and 1771) the most widely read English novels in the South, and usually within a few months of publication. Jefferson had only *Roderick Random* (1748) but many of his contemporaries owned all of the fiction. They also had Henry Brooke's *The Fool of Quality* (1760-1762), said to have been recommended to pious Methodists by John Wesley; Fanny Burney's *Evelina* (1778); William Godwin's *Caleb Williams* (1794), the novel so useful to Poe in the next century; Oliver Goldsmith's *Vicar of Wakefield* (1766); Charlotte Lennox's *The Female Quixote* (1752); Charles Johnstone's *Chrysal, or the Adventures of a Guinea* (1760-1765); and scores of deservedly forgotten Gothic, historical, and sentimental novels imported from Britain. They were also beginning to buy the earliest American fiction in the same genres and the quixotic yet peculiarly American picaresque *Modern Chivalry* (1792-1815) of H. H. Brackenridge. It is harder to determine whether they bought the *Adventures of Alonso* ("By a Native of Maryland," Thomas Atwood Digges), published in London in 1775.

Walter B. Edgar notes in his study of South Carolina colonial libraries that 52 percent of the "literature" in the province was prose fiction. The percentage would surely have been greater had he carried his study to 1800. Another scholar, noting the enormous increase in the novel-reading public in America during the last third of the century, attributes it to the large number of firms in the book trade and the social private, and semipublic circulating libraries. He finds that the fictional titles in booksellers' catalogues were only about 12 percent, but he rightly judges the proportion of novels that were bought to be much greater. His figures are for all America, but two pieces of his evidence come from the South: the ledgers of the bookstore in Williamsburg, Virginia, and the 1801 plea of a bookseller in Raleigh, North Carolina to his wholesaler in Philadelphia for more fiction, "as the good folks here love *light* reading." The accompanying order was entirely for novels. Mason L. Weems, the great salesman who toured the southern coastal area in the last decade of the old century and the first decade of the next, would have agreed.

Not everybody in England or North America read fiction or even approved of reading it; indeed many frowned on the sentimental tales of seduction, incest, and painful death which dominated the market in the late 1780s. This disapproval was as often true, for a variety of reasons, among readers in the Southeast. Before 1760 Samuel Davies is said to have reproached his congregation because they read prose romances instead of the Bible. Yet in 1753 he confided to his diary that he was reading the "Memoirs of the fortunate [Country] Maid, a Romance," which he claimed had a "better" tendency than most of those in vogue. It was the story of the rise of a cottage girl to the rank of marchioness, presumably by retaining her virtue, as Pamela did. It was an English translation of a 1735

French work. The same day he read part of Daniel Defoe's *Roxana, or the Fortunate Mistress* (1724, 1741), "the History of an abandoned Prostitute, pretendedly penitent." These books were read on shipboard, and the good parson was either desperate for reading matter or wanted to find out something about what his parishioners enjoyed. Let it be noted, however, that most of his reading on the voyage to England was not at all frivolous.

Richardson's American admirers were mostly women, if we credit contemporary allusions. William Wirt first heard the plot of *Clarissa* from a female member of the family with whom he boarded in Maryland in 1792 while he attended school, and this was at the age of ten. In 1772 prominent Virginian Wilson Cary ordered handsomely lettered, calf-bound copies of all three of Richardson's novels for his granddaughter Sarah.

Jefferson, who never had many novels in his library, grew less and less fond of them as a genre as the years passed. In his 1771 model-library recommendations to Robert Skipwith he listed Rousseau's *Eloisa*, Johnstone's *Adventures of a Guinea*, two of John Langhorne's romances, Goldsmith's *Vicar*, Brooke's *Fool of Quality*, and the principal fiction of Richardson, Fielding, Smollett, and Sterne. He defended his selections as representing morality and virtue even more strongly than history does. "A well-written Romance" may depict filial duty, for example, more vividly and more effectively than any "dry volumes of ethics, and divinity." A half-century later, in 1818, he decried what he had earlier approved:

A great obstacle to good education is the inordinate passion prevalent for novels, and the time lost in that reading which should be instructively employed. When this passion infects the mind, it destroys it's tone, and revolts it against wholesome reading. . . . the result is a bloated imagination, sickly judgment, and disgust towards the real business of life.

But Jefferson's cause had long since been lost, though (or

perhaps because) in his own region and in America the native
fiction improved (at least in part) in seriousness and artistic
quality. When Jefferson chose the senior professor (who would
be chairman of the faculty) for his new University of Virginia,
he selected a man, George Tucker, who had just published one
of the best of the plantation novels, and who was to spend part
of his first (and it proved to be his last) year with Jefferson,
1825–1826, writing the utopian-antiutopian *A Voyage to the
Moon* (published 1827), which taught public virtue in a manner which the master of Monticello might have approved.

Throughout the eighteenth century the southern American
read the same imaginative and artistic or recreational material
which was available to his American and British contemporaries, and to a considerable extent for the same reasons. If he
differed from the literate outside his region, it was perhaps in a
greater or somewhat different delight in humor and in his
enormous interest in plays. But what seems most significant
about his belletristic reading is the broad spectrum of interest it
represents, and the fact that so many kinds of people of the
upper and middle social classes owned books without discernible professional or political or religious purpose. They had
available in periodicals, newspapers, and books a surprising
range of aesthetic ideas. A recent historian, who, incidentally,
admired southern colonial civilization, has remarked that nowhere else in the history of the Western World has there been
so large a literate, well-read, and sophisticated society which
produced so little of the literature of art, or belles lettres.
Perhaps so. But my observation would be that, even now, if the
present rate of discovery and publication of southern colonial
manuscript material continues, before the end of this century
it may appear that this society produced far more than he
realized.

Conclusion

IN THE FIVE PROVINCIAL GOVERNMENTS OF THE SOUTHEAST IN
the eighteenth century, from the Atlantic coast to the Appalachians, there were more individuals and families who owned
books and read them than has generally been noticed. The
poorest and the least educated usually had the Bible and a
simple commentary or two. The somewhat fuller shelf of the
more learned added another one or two theological volumes,
folios of English statutes, and one or more manuals to aid the
country and county justices, and perhaps a collection of plays
or verse or some sort of history of Great Britain, especially
England.

When one gets beyond the one-shelf inventory—and he may
do so hundreds of times in the period before 1800—he will find
titles that represent a broad spectrum of interests and views.
Law was proportionately far better represented in the larger
libraries than it is today, because every merchant and farmer
and professional man had to protect his economic interests,
which ultimately meant agrarian management or land speculation or taxation, and trained attorneys (until the last decade
or two) were in short supply. The southerner's legal tomes
naturally reflect the problems of his local society, books such as
The Orphan's Legacy. His other legal materials reflect his
views on history and politics.

The historians he read were philosophers and political
theorists, from Herodotus and Polybius and especially Tacitus
to Sir Walter Raleigh and Rapin and Macaulay and Hume. He

interpreted most of them as representing libertarian ideas, the
story of mankind as repeating itself in a series of struggles
against tyranny, the triumph of freedom, and a subsequent
period of decadence in which individual rights were again lost.
From Ralph Wormeley and William Byrd to Jefferson, he
usually saw the past of the Germanic Saxons as an era of
human freedom which was his own natural and rightful heritage. The political commentators he read, from Harrington
and Sidney and Locke through Addison and Trenchard and
Gordon to his pre-Revolutionary and Revolutionary pamph-
leteers, he also saw as champions of individual and New World
liberty against the encroachments of arbitrary power, first
monarchical and then parliamentary. That he read scores of
authors he so interpreted is apparent from the 1701 study of the
government of the plantations in America by an anonymous
Virginian through Jefferson's *Summary View* or Madison's
Federalist papers. But these same tracts, and those of an
avowed royalist like Jonathan Boucher, also reflect certain
conservative social, economic, and even political elements in
some of their reading, as in Addison and Bolingbroke and
Hume. Any historian of the age might expect breadth and a
certain depth in political thinking from the elite of plantation
society, but such a historian may not be prepared for, or at least
aware of, the ubiquity of the politico-historical printed materials a larger number of non-elitest early southerners possessed,
as they appear in their book inventories and in the innumer-
able allusions to them by southern writers in pamphlets and
periodicals and legislative debates.

Religious and theological books and libraries were representative of the major religious trends of the century. The Anglican's theology was strongly tinged with the rationalism and

Latitudinarianism of many of his religious leaders: Tillotson and Hoadly and Wilkins. Individually he may have been brought to mild deism by Wollaston and Joseph Butler and Shaftesbury—if it was deism they advocated. But more often he remained the rationalizing Trinitarian, such as William Byrd or Bishop James Madison, or the nominal Anglican, such as Jefferson and Wythe and Mason, who were reluctant to discuss individual beliefs.

The S.P.G. and its missionaries and libraries through most of the colonial South, the almost universal presence of Allestree's simple devotional manual *The Whole Duty of Man,* and the regular reading of Bunyan's *Pilgrim's Progress* and sermons more pietist than Tillotson's would indicate, however, that the Anglicans were far from given up to atheism or paganism. With their Presbyterian and Baptist brethren, they often owned Calvin's *Institutes,* and they read it—even if only to confute it in printed sermons. From other theological works owned in common by dissenting and Church of England clergy and laity, it is evident that they were usually not too far apart in doctrine. A rector of Charleston's most famous Anglican church wrote the preface for the theological work of an evangelical and dissenting parson.

Presbyterians and Baptists and Quakers were usually evangelical and pietist in the eighteenth century, though the Old Light Presbyterians were not evangelical in Whitefield's sense. The Quakers, Whitefield, and Samuel Davies all aver that they had their greatest success in areas where Anglican clergy—and one should add Anglican religious literature—had not been. That is, they claimed that the inhabitants of Byrd's "Lubberland" throughout the Southeast were hungry for the Christian religion and that they supplied that need. That Quakerism was a strong force in the first half of the century is borne out by their writings and by the Anglican polemical tracts written against them, such as *The Snake in the Grass,* and by the number of books by Friends in Anglican and Presbyterian libraries, or for that matter by such personal religious "experience" as that published by North Carolinian Hermon Husband.

It should appear from this brief survey that the southern clergyman probably possessed as many theological works as his New England contemporary, and that every type of literate southerner owned some of a variety of religious books. But even the Presbyterians in their sermons and tracts and diaries give no indication that they lay in their beds at night cogitating complex theological doctrine. Their libraries almost universally show that they were aware that religion was a part of the life and mind of man, and most of them appear to have been, as Allen Tate alleged of later southerners, convinced supernaturalists, even in the century of reason.

From Maryland to Georgia, Anglicans and most dissenters enjoyed imaginative and creative literature perhaps more than Quaker or Puritan inhibitions allowed their neighbors to the north to do. They read and probably produced plays privately from the beginning of the century, and they enjoyed the public or semiprofessional theater from 1700, though only sporadically at first. Sober Washington and Jefferson and the great Charlestonians were devotees of the theater, and they and their contemporaries owned and read copies of the plays they saw. Tradespeople and apprentice boys perhaps enjoyed the traveling troupes of actors just as much as their social betters. They, as well as Patrick Henry, might quote passages from Addison's *Cato,* which they enjoyed as good drama as well as libertarian politics.

Benjamin Franklin tells us that in Boston apprentices had access to and read *The Spectator* and *The Tatler,* and there is every reason to believe that below the Susquehanna apprentices and indentured servants, as well as almost every literate farmer, merchant, and professional man, enjoyed the polished, witty, character-portraying pages of these periodicals. Though perhaps not one owner in ten read *Gulliver's Travels* for its social or moral or political implications, there is plenty of evidence in provincial newspapers and scattered pamphlets and verse that readers enjoyed it for its satiric comic narrative. By 1750 the sophisticated southerner saw in *Gulliver's Travels* and *A Tale of a Tub* most of what Swift had put in them, but like every generation since, he could read them for recreational pleasure. And Pope's verse in all its qualities appealed to his reason and his fancy.

All the major preromantic poets and fictionists were in many southern collections. Thomson and Young, the sentimental and Gothic novelists, the aestheticians concerned with theories of the beautiful, the sublime, and the grotesque, were not only on the private and circulating library shelves but had worked their way into the pulpit oratory of Samuel Davies, the descriptions of the Natural Bridge and the passage of the Potomac through the Blue Ridge by Thomas Jefferson, and the late-century verses of Thomas Godfrey in North Carolina, Robert Bolling in Virginia, and Joseph Brown Ladd in South Carolina. If, as suggested above, much more than half the books that were bought in the two decades before the end of the century were popular novels, the fact does not mark a lowering of tastes so much as a broadening of the reading public to people who may have read only the Bible—or nothing save perhaps newspapers—before. Inventories of the large libraries of the first quarter of the nineteenth century, for example, were still overwhelmingly titles of nonfiction. But by then every young lady or shop girl carried at least one sentimental romance in her winter muff. She had no library shelf.

The southern colonial and early national bookshelf, one must repeat, grew from the intellectual, religious, and economic needs of an agrarian society. It grew in the Cherokee mountain country, in sea island Georgia, and low-country South Carolina. It probably resembled libraries in the farmhouses or small manor houses of rural England. Its religious nucleus and concomitant volumes on law and history would have seemed natural in a British setting, and the actual titles in the New and the Old World would have been much the same. So would the titles on politics and government, except for what must have been the greater preponderance in southern America of the libertarian. Country squire or plantation owner read much on, and believed in, individual right, but the plantation owner had peculiar problems of representation and taxation, which he felt were most sympathetically discussed by Sidney and Locke and Trenchard and Gordon. He owned and enjoyed belletristic writing with apparently fewer inhibitions than his Pennsylvania or Massachusetts neighbor, and especially the dramatic and the somewhat bawdily satiric. Anticipating one of his region's major contributions to a more mature New World literature was his enjoyment of the British jestbook and tall tale and of contemporary American humor.

Index

Since there are no notes or bibliography, and since this book is concerned with colonial reading and readers, most of the entries are personal names, often followed by book titles (usually abbreviated). The few subject entries are frequently cross-indexed. In order to distinguish colonial books and authors and readers from British or European authors and books, the abbreviation for the name of the colony is placed in parentheses immediately after the name of a colonial author or reader. One may thus assume that unidentified individuals (authors almost always) are not colonial.

Page numbers given for authors or titles usually refer to their presence in libraries. References to evidence of reading of these authors by colonials is usually so designated.